RUDYARD KIPLING

A *Study of the Short Fiction*

Also available in Twayne's Studies in Short Fiction Series

Twayne's Studies in Short Fiction

Gordon Weaver, General Editor
Oklahoma State University

Rudyard Kipling in his study at Naulakha, 1895.
Courtesy of the Library of Congress.

RUDYARD KIPLING

A Study of the Short Fiction

Helen Pike Bauer
Iona College

TWAYNE PUBLISHERS • NEW YORK
Maxwell Macmillan Canada • *Toronto*
Maxwell Macmillan International • *New York Oxford Singapore Sydney*

Twayne's Studies in Short Fiction No. 58

Twayne Publishers   Maxwell Macmillan Canada, Inc.
Macmillan Publishing Company   1200 Eglinton Avenue East
866 Third Avenue   Suite 200
New York, New York 10022   Don Mills, Ontario M3C 3N1

Library of Congress Cataloging-in-Publication Data
Bauer, Helen Pike.
    Rudyard Kipling : a study in short fiction / Helen Pike Bauer.
        p.   cm.—(Twayne's studies in short fiction ; no. 58)
    Includes bibliographical references (p.) and index.
    ISBN 0-8057-8345-8
    1. Kipling, Rudyard, 1865-1936—Criticism and interpretation.
    2. Short story.   I. Title.   II. Series.
    PR4857.B38   1994
    823' .8—dc20   94-6829
                                                                        CIP

10 9 8 7 6 5 4 3 2 1

Printed in the United States of America.

*For Stephen,
Elizabeth, and Anne*

Contents

Preface

Rudyard Kipling's biography lends itself to clear units and divisions. Born in Bombay in 1865, the son of an English artist and teacher, John Lockwood Kipling, and his wife, Alice, Rudyard lived the happy, comfortable childhood of an Anglo-Indian, a term that, at that time, meant an English man, woman, or child living in India. In 1871, he was, like many such children of his generation, sent back to England to be educated. For five desperately unhappy years, he and his sister boarded in an English home; for the rest of his life, Kipling looked back on this time as grueling and dispiriting. The intelligent, articulate, lively boy was bullied, punished, and humiliated by a provincial, gloomily religious family. Released from his burdensome environment when his parents learned of his unhappiness, Kipling became a student at the United Services College, a school that trained English boys for civil service positions. Although they never intended him for such work, Kipling's parents, who were not wealthy, could afford the college, a less expensive institution than the typical boarding school. In 1882, Kipling's father found him a job on a newspaper in India, and the sixteen year old returned to the land of his birth to become a journalist.

From 1882 until 1889, he worked first on the *Civil and Military Gazette* and later on the *Pioneer*, two newspapers edited by Anglo-Indians and directed to that community. He wrote prolifically—newspaper reports, short travel articles, short stories, and verse. During these years he established his reputation throughout the Anglo-Indian community as a remarkably gifted young writer. In 1889, hoping to launch an international career, he returned to England. Within a few years, he had indeed established a brilliant reputation.

In 1892, he married an American and moved to Vermont, where he continued to write, largely about India and England. He returned to England in 1896 to make his home there. But he traveled widely, especially to South Africa, where he wintered and wrote about contemporary conditions and the Boer War. In England he was vocal about world events and wrote and lectured increasingly about the rise of

Germany and World War I. During these active public years, he continued to write and publish great quantities of poetry and fiction. Though his reputation among literary critics diminished, he received many formal honors, refusing the poet laureateship but accepting the Nobel Prize for Literature in 1907. He died in 1936.

One can neatly organize Kipling's biography geographically—his years in India, in England, in America, in South Africa. And, at first glance, these categories might seem to correspond to different groups of short stories, those set in India or in England, for example. But, looking more closely, one sees that Kipling wrote about India all his life; almost exclusively in his youth, to be sure, but many years after he returned to England for good, he was still looking back to India and reexamining the imperial experience. So, too, he began writing of England early in his career, interspersing, in the 1890s, English with Indian settings. In general, the Indian settings diminish as Kipling grows older; the English settings increase. But dividing his output simply along geographical lines can present interpretive problems.

Neither can one examine Kipling merely as a writer who improved as he grew more experienced. Many of his earlier stories are compelling—short, succinct, dramatic, complete—though others are negligible and ephemeral. His later stories tend to be more complex in structure, more intricate in development. Many of these are rich, evocative, memorable, but others are obscure, convoluted, and flat. Kipling's style may have changed somewhat as he grew older, but this change is not necessarily a mark of either developing or diminishing artistic ability.

It is more profitable, perhaps, to search Kipling's work for a handful of concerns, thematic and aesthetic, that seemed to occupy him persistently throughout his career. While noting that these concerns may take different forms when they appear in different settings, with different subjects, they nevertheless seem to represent important matters to Kipling, important aspects of human life, critical moral problems; important aspects of narrative art, strategies and techniques. Focusing on these concerns, while paying attention to the way they develop as Kipling grows older, may help bring the reader closer to the true Kipling experience.

It is commonplace in discussions of Kipling to note the dramatic changes in his reputation. Acclaimed in his youth, he began to fall in critical esteem in the early twentieth century. His political views, always deeply held and vehemently stated, became less popular. The

English at home had become more ambivalent about the Empire than those who had traveled out to India to serve in the army or government. And the Boer War, which Kipling enthusiastically supported, was opposed by many in England. He came to be seen as the apologist for a discredited imperialism. The 1890s, moreover, had seen the beginnings of a literature very foreign to his sensibility, the work of Hardy, Wilde, George Moore, and Yeats, for example, writers developing in directions of subject matter and style that Kipling would not or could not follow. By the time England entered World War I, Kipling, to many, had come to seem aesthetically old-fashioned, politically outmoded, intellectually coarse, vulgar, brutal.

But Kipling, then as now, always maintained a loyal band of readers. Many of his almost four hundred short stories and two of his three novels have been continually reprinted, always available and popular. For among his concerns are some that perpetually interest readers of literature. He frequently examines the lives of men and women under extreme circumstances: in a limited and artificial colonial society; in an isolated, obscure outpost, the sole representative of embattled Western values; at war; on the homefront during war; after the death of a beloved child; as the one human being in a community of animals. Exploring character under confusion, ambivalence, and stress, Kipling tests the power of the human commitment to value, the power of private virtue and its relationship to civilization. He repeatedly places characters at the axis where physical and psychic survival intersect with allegiance to socially approved values and sees both the precariousness of those values and, simultaneously, man's dependence on them to provide a defense against the disintegration of the unsupported personality.

Among those stories that have insured Kipling's popularity with a large group of readers are his treatments of childhood, especially those stories in the Jungle Books that trace the intellectual and emotional growth of Mowgli, the boy raised by wolves. The particular flavor of these stories, their blend of natural history and mythopoesis, their affectionate, humorous tone mingled with a realistic appraisal of animal life, have made them popular with children and adults. But in these tales, too, Kipling weighs the informing power of social structure on individual personality. While giving the jungle animals who rear Mowgli a large measure of emotion, intellect, and moral value, Kipling insists on the distinction between the animal and the human. Mowgli possesses a nascent imaginative power and intellectual authority unavailable to his jungle guardians and friends. These innate gifts and the inevitable allegiance to the human world that they portend are immediately recognized by the animals. It is Mowgli's growing comprehension of his condition that gives pathos to the stories. Their powerful impact derives in part from this mingling of intellectual considerations and emotional consequences.

Kipling's other stories of childhood, too, often focus on the tension between the protagonist's character struggling to emerge and the powerful influence of circumstances with which that character must contend. The psychic buffeting a young child must undergo as he moves from one group of companions to another can either strengthen or undermine the fragile personality. Kipling's stories of children are sometimes accused of being sentimental, and some of them are, but the best are acute in their understanding of childhood's struggles and resonant in their indications of the private and social significance of these dangers.

It is in his children's stories, both those about the child Mowgli and those *Just So Stories* written for his own children, that Kipling's fabulist imagination is best known. But his delight in giving human qualities where they do not exist extends to imbuing machines with life. Kipling has a great number of stories tracing the thoughts and emotions of animals and objects; some of these are easily read as allegorical of man's life, others less so. But all reveal an imagination that saw a mysterious unity in all existence.

If the pains of childhood are a concern in many of Kipling's short stories, particularly those of his middle years, one form of adult sorrow occurs repeatedly in the later stories, the death of a loved one and the protagonist's struggle to accept that loss. Kipling is often thought of as a war writer, one who focuses frequently on men in battle, whether the border skirmishes of Anglo-India, the clashes of the Boer War, or the fierce violence of World War I. But, particularly as he grows older, Kipling focuses not so much on those who fight as on those who remain at home, waiting for word of their loved one's fate. Again and again in the later stories, sometimes in the context of war, sometimes not, Kipling treats those whose most beloved has died. He examines the effect of such profound loss on character and value. A protagonist may be permanently damaged by the loss, overwhelmed by grief and the desire for revenge, or, more frequently, may find the confrontation with that loss a means for plumbing his own character. Kipling's stories of grief and the need for emotional healing are among his most touching and, for many modern critics, his most successful.

The decline into which Kipling's reputation fell during his lifetime intensified after his death. Positive responses to his work rarely made their way into print. Indeed, the academic establishment seemed to dismiss him; few professional studies were published. Yet, an occasional noted writer, T. S. Eliot or Edmund Wilson or Randall Jarrell, would produce a long, sophisticated though ambivalent evaluation of Kipling's work.[1] Recent years, however, have seen a vigorous new interest in that work, as evidenced by a plethora of new paperback collections of his short stories, as well as new editions of his letters and his autobiography, and new collections of the reminiscences of his friends.[2] The raw material for a critical reevaluation of Kipling's work is being provided. Simultaneously, a handful of critics have begun that reevaluation. There are new full-length analytical studies, as well as entire issues of scholarly journals devoted to Kipling's work. There has been a new collection of the major interpretive responses to his work.[3] Kipling will probably never regain the near-unanimous approval he once enjoyed, but there are many aspects of his writing that have begun to be appreciated anew.

Modern critics looking at Kipling's stories are finding there a treatment of questions and problems that is more subtle, complex, and intelligent than had often been previously credited. They focus on the ambiguous, fantastic, or obscure in Kipling's fiction, aspects that mitigate against a simplistic reading of the stories. John Bayley discusses the tension between Kipling's oft-stated desire to treat "things-as-they-are" and the mystery or opacity of his stories.[4] And, Bayley concludes, the overt moral of Kipling's stories often sits uneasily with the almost magical quality of his imagination. Part of Kipling's dealing with life's complexity and ambiguity is indirect, a result of narrative technique, the use of an unreliable or at least unknowable narrator. This modern critical focus on the narrator is in sharp contrast to earlier treatments of the short stories where commentators identified Kipling with his narrator; one critic went so far as to consistently call the narrator "Kipling." In other stories, Kipling works more overtly with the problem of knowing the truth of a situation; incidents may be left ambiguously resolved or interpreted; at times, the impossibility of conclusive knowledge becomes the very point of a story. This concern of Kipling's, which he often phrases in terms of people never fully understanding each other, places him more fully in the modern temper and has led some critics to reevaluate earlier assumptions about Kipling's unequivocal enthusiasm for imperialism.

So too his focus on the role of language in understanding or misunderstanding has attracted contemporary critics. Particularly in his Indian stories, the division between human beings is seen as an inability of the speaker of one language ever to understand fully the mind of one who speaks another. Language is not a transparent medium but a structure that determines what can be said, indeed, what can be thought; the structure of one language will not correspond completely with that of another. Kipling's well-known belief that divisions between races are almost impossible to overcome is gradually being revealed as more than simply the European's sense of superiority over the non-European and is beginning to be seen as a serious treatment of the profound effects that language and custom have on people's thought and character. Indeed, Elliot L. Gilbert argues that the discrepancy between reality and language in Kipling is philosophical; Kipling, he states, believes that reality cannot be reached by language; the most profound response a character may have to his or her experience is silence.[5]

Another aspect of Kipling's work that is undergoing a reevaluation is his verbal artistry. From the beginning, Kipling was seen as a masterful storyteller, appreciated for his skill in structuring and pacing a tale, his ability to capture a character in a few salient details. More recently, critics have acknowledged the sheer beauty of his language, his long evocative descriptions and lush visual detail. The importance of the visual arts in Kipling's life has been well-known; his father was an artist, professor of architectural sculpture, and museum curator. Kipling spent many childhood vacations at the home of his aunt Georgiana and her husband, the Pre-Raphaelite painter Sir Edward Burne-Jones. Kipling himself illustrated the *Just So Stories*. But the impact that this artistic bent had on his writing is only beginning to be acknowledged. And one mark of recent criticism is how often a particular painter's work is invoked as an analogy for Kipling's style. New attention is being paid too to Kipling's frequent use of art as a metaphor. A number of stories trace the work of the artist, the process of art, providing insights into Kipling's beliefs about his own work and the role of art in society.

A fresh look at Kipling, then, demands that one consider those aspects of his work that have been permanently part of his attraction as a writer, his vivid evocations of exotic settings, his compelling treatments of men and women in crisis, his understanding of the stresses and delights of childhood, and his ability to capture them in a fabulist mode. But one must also consider qualities of Kipling's work that are being newly revealed or reevaluated, his complex narrative line; his ironic, ambivalent tone; his poetic language.

The number of Kipling's short stories is daunting, almost four hundred. One cannot hope to discuss all or even most of them; to do so would create a study that looked like an annotated list of titles. In the essay that follows I attempt, instead, to locate some important concerns and techniques in Kipling's work and illustrate them in a developed discussion of some of the major short stories. I extend and supplement these discussions with briefer treatments of some major, and at times minor, tales. What one generation deems minor, of course, another often considers major, and these lines are always being redrawn. I will leave it to the reader, in persuing his or her own study of Kipling, to come upon still other stories that enrich an understanding of his sensibility and artistry. One advantage of reading such a prolific writer is that the student, from the newest to the most seasoned, always has the happy opportunity of discovering a new story.

Notes to Part 1

1. See T. S. Eliot, "Introduction," in *A Choice of Kipling's Verse* (London: Faber and Faber, 1941); Edmund Wilson, "The Kipling that Nobody Read," in *The Wound and the Bow* (New York: Oxford University Press, 1947); and Randall Jarrell, "On Preparing to Read Kipling," "In the Vernacular," "The English in England," in *Kipling, Auden & Co.: Essays and Reviews, 1935–1964* (New York: Farrar, Strauss and Giroux, 1980).

2. Both Oxford University Press and Penguin Books, for example, have published during the 1980s new paperback editions of most of Kipling's major short-story collections. See also *The Letters of Rudyard Kipling*, ed. Thomas Pinney, 2 vols. (Iowa City: University of Iowa Press, 1990); Rudyard Kipling, *Something of Myself and Other Autobiographical Writings*, ed. Thomas Pinney (Cambridge: Cambridge University Press, 1990)—hereafter cited in the text; and Harold Orel, ed., *Kipling: Interviews and Recollections*, 2 vols. (Totowa, N.J.: Barnes and Noble Books, 1983).

3. A groundbreaking modern study is Elliot L. Gilbert's *The Good Kipling: Studies in the Short Story* (Oberlin: Ohio University Press, 1970); hereafter cited in the text. Some more recent studies include John A. McClure, *Kipling and Conrad: The Colonial Fiction* (Cambridge: Harvard University Press, 1981); Sandra Kemp, *Kipling's Hidden Narratives* (London: Basil Blackwell, 1988);

Nora Crook, *Kipling's Myths of Love and Death* (Basingstoke: Macmillan Press, 1989); Mark Paffard, *Kipling's Indian Fiction* (Basingstoke: Macmillan Press, 1989); and *English Literature in Transition, 1880–1920* 29 (1986) devoted Numbers 1 and 2 to essays on Kipling. For recent collections of critical essays, see Harold Orel, ed., *Critical Essays on Rudyard Kipling* (Boston: G. K. Hall, 1989), and Philip Mallett, ed., *Kipling Considered* (Basingstoke: Macmillan Press, 1989).

4. John Bayley, "The False Structure," *English Literature in Transition, 1880–1920* 29 (1986): 19–27.

5. Elliot L. Gilbert, "Silence and Survival in Rudyard Kipling's Art and Life," *English Literature in Transition, 1880–1920* 29 (1986): 115–26.

Acknowledgments

Kipling's speeches "Literature" and "Fiction," copyright 1928 by Rudyard Kipling, are used by permission of Doubleday, a division of Bantam Doubleday Dell Publishing Group, Inc.

Excerpts from *Something of Myself* by Rudyard Kipling, copyright 1937 by Caroline Kipling, are used by permission of Doubleday, a division of Bantam Doubleday Dell Publishing Group, Inc.

An excerpt from John A. McClure's *Kipling and Conrad: The Colonial Fiction* is reprinted by permission of the publishers (Cambridge, Mass.: Harvard University Press), copyright 1981 by the President and Fellows of Harvard College.

An excerpt from Clare Hanson's *Short Stories and Short Fictions, 1880–1980*, copyright Clare Hanson 1985, is reprinted with permission of St. Martin's Press, Incorporated.

I am pleased to thank Iona College for providing me with a year-long faculty fellowship, during which most of the research and much of the writing of this study was completed. I thank my colleagues in the English department whose support and encouragement were much appreciated. I thank too Ryan Library of Iona College, which has been most efficient in its interlibrary loan services.

I am grateful to the New York Public Library, Astor, Lenox, and Tilden Foundations for its extensive holdings and the helpfulness of its staff.

Mickey Pearlman, erstwhile colleague, always friend, helped initiate this project and cheered it on. For this, and many other good deeds, I thank her.

My deepest debt is acknowledged in the dedication to this study.

Part 1

THE SHORT FICTION

"The Dread Meaning of Loneliness"

In his earliest stories, Kipling takes as his major subject the experience of being an Anglo-Indian. He treats the lives of soldiers, their struggle for survival, for promotion, for companionship; the routine of civil servants, their sense of duty, their fatigues and small pleasures; the dilemmas of wives and children seeking to make a new life in a foreign land. He even presents on occasion the perspective of the Indian, whose home has been profoundly altered by European imperialism. And he develops his subjects in many moods, admiring, cynical, and jocular. But he focuses within these diverse stories on what he considers the distinguishing qualities of the Anglo-Indian life: the confronting of an alien culture about which one knows very little; the sense of superiority bred of being a colonizing power; the psychological claustrophobia induced by being part of a narrow, closely knit, inescapable social circle; the danger of living in a land often beset by small regional conflicts and border skirmishes; the omnipresent threat of illness and death in an environment of crowding, intense heat, and uncertain sanitation; the isolation of daily living in a remote outpost. From this complex of conditions Kipling creates a thematic concern. In "At the End of the Passage" he terms it "the dread meaning of loneliness," and to some degree it would occupy him for the rest of his career.[1]

To be sure, Kipling does not often describe what J. M. S. Tompkins calls "the abyss"[2]; more often he describes his characters' attempts to avoid it or compensate for it. But in a handful of stories one can see what Kipling's characters fear, and the first descriptions are in the Indian stories. It is not just physical isolation, though that is often part of it, but the physical is more the occasion than the experience itself. Being removed from others leads one into a habit of mind; one begins to question, or distrust, or see through those values that society constructs for us all and that we ordinarily so unthinkingly accept—political values, social values, moral values. One looks and sees nothing that endures; everything, even the self, comes to seem contingent, brittle, and hollow.

"At the End of the Passage" is one of Kipling's most developed and frightening treatments of this perception of nothingness, here so profound it ends in madness and death. The story begins by describing how four Anglo-Indians—a physician, a civil servant, a surveyor, and an engineer—each of whom fulfills a minor role in the Empire, meet weekly for a card game and dinner. Though they do not particularly like each other, the men depend on each other for the routine of conversation and cards. The intense heat they endure and the inherent futility of the work they carry out combine with isolation and enervating boredom to make their lives almost unbearable. Still, when the engineer, Hummil, speculates that his subordinate's death may have been a suicide and that no behavior should be condemned in this climate, "I judge no man this weather," the others reject such a solution. As the physician, Spurstow, says laconically, "suicide is shirking your work." If this reason seems weak to the reader, to these men it is the strongest and best they have.

Kipling compares the atmosphere in which the men live to hell, a metaphor he introduces in the verse he uses as an epigraph.

> The sky is lead and our faces are red,
> And the Gates of Hell are opened and riven,
> And the winds of Hell are loosened and driven,
> And the dust flies up in the face of Heaven.

The men's attempts to escape, through work or friendship, seem doomed. At one point, Mottram, the surveyor, sings an old hymn, tinkling an out-of-tune piano. The others grow silent and nostalgic, but Kipling insists that the small place of refuge they are trying to create through ritual and memory is overwhelmed by their daily lives. Hummil breaks the silence, "you sing it when you are seven fathom deep in Hell! It's an insult to the intelligence of the Deity to pretend we're anything but tortured rebels."

This story, which is largely a study in atmosphere, ends in death. Exhausted, Hummil keeps seeing a vision of himself, sitting at table or gliding through his rooms. Moreover, he has been driven to insomnia because, beset by nightmares, he is afraid to sleep. The others finally discover his body, blank eyes staring into the face of an imagined demon, "a blind face that cries and can't wipe its eyes." Kipling has been accused of being melodramatic in his conclusion, but his suggestion that Hummil's dead eyes retain the image of his nightmare, an image that can be photographed and seen by others, suggests not only his lifelong interest in the mysterious and inexplicable but his habit of solidifying, even corporealizing, those mental states that frighten men. The things we most fear can literally rise up to haunt us. The technique becomes more prominent in the later stories, but appears in those as early as "The Phantom 'Rickshaw" (*PR*) and "The Strange Ride of Morrowbie Jukes" (*PR*), locating these tales in a region somewhere between nightmare and conscious obsession.

The vivid setting and its psychological consequences developed in "At the End of the Passage" capture some of the most persistent elements in Kipling's treatment of despair: the solitude of the isolated outpost, the value but limitations of comradeship, and the gradual breakdown of a human being beset by physical privation and mental strain. Hummil, companionless for six out of every seven days, broken by the heat and illness of an Indian summer, prevented by a sense of duty from leaving his job, faces only suffering and hallucination. None of the comforts in which he had been taught to place his trust, not the efficacy of work or the solace of friends, can defeat his demons. And he chooses even death not in peace but in panic. Hummil represents a humanity driven beyond its limits, a man who can find no release, not even in oblivion.

In "The Madness of Private Ortheris" (*PTH*), Kipling treats many of these same elements but in a lighter tone. Ortheris, the Anglo-Indian soldier, is subject to bouts of homesickness so intense that he loses awareness of his duties and the ability to control his actions. He complains vociferously about his life and is about to desert when he recovers himself, "the devils" depart, and he returns to his company. His protective friend, Mulvaney, and the narrator have been prepared to trick Ortheris into reason, but their stratagems are not necessary. Yet the reader knows that Ortheris's fit will return. His homesickness has been beaten back but not defeated, and the usual support of friends can only hope to provide a temporary stay.

Still another of Kipling's early Indian stories, "Thrown Away" (*PTH*), explores the breakdown of a personality under isolation, but here from a different vantage point, that of a third-person narrator, experienced, knowing, even cynical. The tale is of a young man, never given a name but referred to simply as The Boy, who is sent out to the Anglo-Indian military, inexperienced and innocent about the world. His naivete leaves him with no standards by which to judge the Indian experience. "There was a Boy once who had been brought up under the 'sheltered life' theory; and the theory killed him dead." Oversensitive to praise and blame, overindulgent in amusements and quarrels, The Boy, without guidance or perspective, shoots himself. Although it is the Indian climate and society that form the immediate scene for the story, the anonymity of The Boy, indeed of all the characters, gives them a universal dimension. Kipling's narrator argues that only serious preparation and a clear-eyed, tough stance can confront the hardness of life. The Boy had hardly begun to see the worst that India could give; his weakness destroyed him at the first blow.

The story judges, too, the importance of comrades. In life, The Boy had none; his isolation was critical. But the narrator and the Major, who too late intuit The Boy's suicidal intentions and find his body, know that his sheltered English family could not bear learning of the moral deterioration of their son. The experienced Anglo-Indians concoct a story: The Boy died of cholera, a lie not so much to protect the dead as the living. The Boy was destroyed by his innocence; the narrator and the Major are trying to keep the English family from being destroyed by theirs. The ending of the story, the apparent success of the lie, suggests one attitude toward the Anglo-Indian adventure often detectible in Kipling's stories: only those who have lived in India can begin to understand the toll it takes; the English at home, either believing a romanticized national version of imperialism or unthinkingly opposing its professed aims, have no conception of the strain and privation, the moral complexities, the confused allegiances that the English in India endure. The occasional MP who comes out on a political junket to visit India is a frequent butt of Kipling's humor. But Kipling more often treats the English ignorance of Indian reality in sober terms. When he returned to England, Kipling saw the political consequences of such a lack of understanding; in his Indian tales, he traces the human consequences.

But in one of his earliest stories, "The Strange Ride of Morrowbie Jukes," first published when he was twenty years old, Kipling examines the breakdown of values undergone by the central character, not because of prolonged physical isolation, or emotional immaturity, or the failure of Anglo-Indian society to support his morale. Rather, Jukes has grown dependent on just those structures that the Anglo-Indian world provides. He cannot endure their removal. Morrowbie Jukes, an English civil engineer working in India, in a frenzy induced by illness and fever, rides his horse out one night and falls into a deep crater of sand. Unable to scale the crumbling walls, he finds himself trapped with a group of Indians who live in a world of the half-dead, condemned to spend their remaining days and years in this grim pit because they had escaped their own death by surviving their bungled cremations. They no longer belong to the world of ordinary human society; they are family-less, caste-less. Yet these forsaken, miserable creatures still cling to life; they trap crows for food, quarrel among themselves, and warily avoid the various guards and natural traps that stand against escape.

At first Jukes responds to his plight by using the rational tools of the Western administrator; he estimates the size of the crater, the slope of the hill, the measurements of the numerous burrows that pockmark the surface. But his attempt to control his environment by accumulating knowledge about it proves ludicrously futile. He learns the truth about his fate only when he meets Gunga Dass, a junior government worker Jukes had known years before, now one of the wretched natives who inhabit this pit of despair.

But it is not the physical deprivation that Jukes finds most intolerable; it is his loss of status. He, an Anglo-Indian, expects to be treated deferentially, but in this domain of the lost all are equal. At first Jukes merely resents the insolence the others display toward him. He states pompously, "even in these days, when local self-government has destroyed the greater part of a native's respect for a Sahib, I have been accustomed to a certain amount of civility from my inferiors, and on approaching the crowd naturally expected that there would be some recognition of my presence. As a matter of fact there was, but it was by no means what I had looked for. The ragged crew actually laughed at me—such laughter I hope I may never hear again." His easy assumptions about his innate superiority are not shared by the others; in fact, it is Gunga Dass, knowledgeable about this new life, who provides leadership. And Jukes, who despises the degradation, the ugly scramble for survival that he sees around him, finds himself, in fear, reduced to the same behavior. In this surreal world, Jukes literally eats crow, threatens murder, panics and throws himself to the ground, screaming and shivering. He exhibits the marks of behavioral inferiority he had associated with the natives. But this is a world where the hierarchical structures of authority no longer obtain. "I had left the world, it seemed, for centuries. I was as certain then as I am now of my own existence, that in the accursed settlement there was no law save that of the strongest, that the living dead men had thrown behind them every canon of the world which had cast them out; and that I had to depend for my own life on my strength and vigilance alone." And he adds ominously, "the crew of the ill-fated *Mignonette* are the only men who would understand my frame of mind." In 1884, three crew members of the shipwrecked *Mignonette* had been convicted of murdering and eating a cabin boy to survive. Jukes identifies himself with those who have broken the greatest taboo, cannibalism.

A faithful servant who has followed the tracks of Jukes's horse finally rescues the desperate man, but not before Jukes has witnessed the collapse of those values by which he has lived. Removed from the society that sustained those values, the traditions of social hierarchy and comradeship, the imperialist's training to lead and yet protect his subordinates, the assurance of a stable system on which he could unthinkingly depend, all evaporate. Men are reduced to hungry animals fighting over a dead crow, howling in fear. Kipling's pit of sand has been aptly compared to Dante's Inferno.[3] What sustains Kipling's Anglo-India is not God's grace, however, but man's institutions. When they vanish, chaos reigns. It has been argued that Jukes's experience demonstrates the fragility of the Anglo-Indian personality, sustained as it must be by the structures of the Empire. Critics have seen the story as an allegory of the hollowness of the Empire itself, founded on racism and the desire for domination; the English, though imposing their will and power on Indian life, remain ignorant of the land and culture they inhabit. And Jukes's story explodes the myth of Empire, reveals its essential instability and fraudulence. The English hegemony is reduced to impotence.[4]

But "At the End of the Passage" and "The Strange Ride of Morrowbie Jukes" can also be read as any human being's relationship to his or her society, an exploration of society's importance in creating and maintaining an individual's values and sanity. Deprived of companionship and the voices that echo one's assumptions, deprived of political and social status, a human being loses those props that give order and coherence to daily life. Physical and psychological loneliness, then, so much a part of Kipling's portrayal of Anglo-India, is a state that remains in Kipling's vision a fundamental and undeniable aspect of human life. Anglo-India, with its particular geographic and cultural conditions, provides a powerful locus for exploring man's fear of isolation and abandonment. But Kipling returns to this theme repeatedly in his career, after the Anglo-Indian tales most powerfully perhaps in his stories of World War I, particularly those that deal with the state generally termed shell shock. In these stories Kipling focuses on two aspects of war that wreak the most havoc: the bizarre and disorienting sights and sounds, and the obliteration of the normal standards of behavior. Kipling's soldiers, in a world of noise, smoke, and stench, their minds unable to construct coherent images of physical reality, find their moral values distorted as well, their assurances snatched away, their assumptions no longer trustworthy.

In "A Friend of the Family" (*D&C*), a group of veterans meets, each man remembering his experiences in war. One old soldier demonstrates how private moral chaos can result from the confrontation with public chaos, the irrationality of war. "There's a limit to what you can stand. It takes all men differently. Noise was what started me, at last. I'd got just up to the edge—wonderin' when I'd crack an' how many of our men I'd do in if it came on me while we were busy. I had that nice taste in the mouth and the nice temperature they call trench-fever, an'—I had to feel inside my head for the meanin' of every order I gave or was responsible for executin'." The mind of Bevin, the speaker, had been confused by war; he could no longer follow orders without retranslating them for himself. But more alarming, his morality was confused as well; he felt it was only a matter of time before he turned his gun on his comrades. Now, in their postwar life, Bevin and another soldier discuss the reasons why life after the war seems unstable and unsatisfactory. "The trouble is, there hasn't been any judgment taken or executed. That's why the world is where it is now. We didn't need anything but justice—afterwards. Not gettin' that, the bottom fell out of things, naturally."

For these are simple men who assumed the justice of the cause they were fighting for. But the war did not provide justice; the deprivation and horror they encountered culminated in nothing satisfactory. "A Friend of the Family" ends with arson and destruction, an attempt to wreak a private justice under the camouflage of war. A man's personal revenge is carried out by his making the explosion look like the result of enemy bombing. The values and methods of war are extrapolated into private life. War becomes not only the training ground for later life; the values it annihilates can never be recovered.

In one of his last tales, "The Tender Achilles" (*L&R*), Kipling recounts the story of Wilkett, a brilliant medical researcher who volunteers to use his knowledge by serving as a surgeon at the battlefront. Poorly prepared for this work, consumed by guilt at his inadequacy, driven, exhausted, appalled by the physical horrors he must confront, Wilkett breaks down. He had placed his trust in science and hard work, but they do not suffice. The chaos outside and within defeat him, and, racked by psychosomatic pain, he returns home. The narrator and his colleagues, also physicians, contrive to restore Wilkett by a hoax, and they succeed. But the reader is left, even after Wilkett's decision to return to research, with the portrait of a man broken by war and by doubt. The confident ending of the story never erases that image.

But perhaps the most successful and haunting of Kipling's treatments of war not merely as the cause but as the arena of man's confrontation with that which undermines and destroys his easy complacency, his accepting of order at face value, is "A Madonna of the Trenches" (*D&C*). The young soldier, Strangwick, is ostensibly the victim of shell shock; he cannot forget the piles of frozen French bodies, stacked high, used as barriers in the trenches. He obsessively hears them creak as they defrost; he rehearses his pounding them back in line and covering them over so they will continue to protect the living. But, as horrific as Strangwick's memories of the physical condition of the trenches are, the true cause of his breakdown lies elsewhere. He has glimpsed a world beyond the war; an old family friend, who is Strangwick's military superior, has made a suicide pact with Strangwick's aunt. The young soldier discovers, to his horror, the apparition of his aunt, on the day of her death, looking with sexual longing at "Uncle John," drawing him into a gas-heated hut where they will make love and die together, confident that they will enter eternity in each other's arms, never to be separated. Strangwick's glimpse into this world, so foreign to that he knows, a world of intense, illicit love undimmed by years of separation, a world where hope for the resurrection of the body is fueled by physical desire, where the spiritual is at one with the profane, so shocks the young soldier's confidence in the rational, quotidian world he has known that even the horrors of war pale by comparison. The *liebestod* he has witnessed defies the mundane, and he can return to neither the explanations nor the values of a world that once made sense. He gives up his old girlfriend, "she don't know what reel things mean. *I* do. . . . The reel thing's life an' death." The story ends with Strangwick still wandering in a world that does not conform to what he knows to be true: life's most intense experiences transcend our artificial categories of life and death, right and wrong; the boundaries that separate the physical from the spiritual can be broken through, and the rare souls endowed with such power find themselves in joy and peace. But

Strangwick, the mere spectator, is in misery, "me soul turned over inside me because—because it knocked out everything I'd believed in. I'ad nothin' to lay 'old of, d'ye see?"

So many of Kipling's stories, then, from the earliest Anglo-Indian to the last war tales, deal with a character, usually a man, who by physical privation and isolation, by social, psychological, or moral loneliness finds himself staring into an abyss. What he sees there may be emptiness or the something that annihilates all he formerly believed; it may traumatize him; it may even kill him; at the very least it leaves him permanently altered, no longer able to accept the world's conventional judgments, no longer amenable to facile rewards and consolations.

One story that has been studied by critics looking for a deeper understanding of this chord in Kipling's work is the directly autobiographical "Baa, Baa, Black Sheep" (*WWW*).[5] These readers have tried to ascertain the degree of heightening, of artistry, in the tale. How true is it to Kipling's real experience? There is no doubt that the story reveals Kipling's mature powers: in its vivid characterizations, assured pacing, dramatic scenes, poetic language, and particularly in the many ways it corresponds to the literary tradition of nineteenth-century treatments of child-victims. And yet the suffering and anger at the core of the tale suggest a personal bond between Kipling and the life of the young protagonist akin to Dickens's with David Copperfield. Indeed, the bare facts of the story, the plot, the personalities of those involved, the atmosphere that clothes the events, have been corroborated by Kipling's sister, Trix, his companion during the years the story covers.[6]

When he was five years old, Rudyard Kipling and his younger sister were sent back to England to be educated, just as the central characters, the boy, Punch, and his sister, Judy, are sent in "Baa, Baa, Black Sheep." The two fictional children, accompanied by their parents, arrive to board at Downe Lodge on the south coast of England. The children have been told nothing of what would transpire; they assume this to be a temporary stop on a family trip. But they awaken one morning a few days after their arrival to discover that their parents have left. At first the children trust that their beloved parents will return. But as the days lengthen and their guardians, the tyrannical and violent Antirosa, her bullying son, and her kindly but ineffectual husband, reiterate that they are alone now, the children first fight against and then accept their fate. Antirosa, an Evangelical fanatic, lectures

Punch that his parents have abandoned him because he is so consumed by sin. But Punch's own meager understanding perceives a more mysterious universe. He does not know why he suffers so, but he is aware that he has lost the paradise of his infancy.

"Baa, Baa, Black Sheep" locates, for Kipling, the nadir of human experience. Inexplicably cast out from a loving world, undeservedly despised and tormented, renamed "Black Sheep" to epitomize his distance from everything his guardians value, the child can find no sense or succor. Even his cherished sister has been unaccountably accepted and petted by Antirosa. Punch, in self-defense, turns to lying and cheating, but these bring only more punishment. His only relief is reading, an escape through imagination. The world around him, both mundane and spiritual, merely tortures him. Antirosa's God is no refuge; He is painted as an omniscient punisher. The life that stretches before Punch is unrelenting loneliness and despair.

Five years after arriving at Downe Lodge, Punch is finally reclaimed by his family. But in some ways it is too late. His eyesight has been permanently damaged by physiological weakness and medical neglect. But, more important, the psychological effects of his experience, the confrontation with incomprehensible abandonment, with irrational brutality, petty spite, and jealousy have wrought ineradicable marks on the boy. Kipling concludes his story: "when young lips have drunk deep of the bitter waters of Hate, Suspicion, and Despair, all the Love in the world will not wholly take away that knowledge."

"Baa, Baa, Black Sheep" examines the mind of the young child in rich detail. Kipling describes Punch's responses to the vagaries of his experience, from the affectionate bedtime rituals he performs with his nurse in India to his stumbling, half-blind and beaten, through the cold English parlor at Downe Lodge. But the specificity of description does not mitigate the story's almost archetypal quality, the simplicity of its characters and plot: the loving but missing parents, the cruel guardians, the persecuted child. These might lead one to read the story as a study in the child's fear of abandonment. But the psychological pattern that is developed—the secure world that cannot be trusted, the plunge into hell, the exchange of familiar behavior and values for the incomprehensible, the impotence of the protagonist to alter his fate except for the worse, the loneliness even when surrounded by others—all these are central to Kipling's work as a whole. That he underwent some such experience as a child is undeniable. To say that his experience has been heightened and dramatized is only to say that it has been retold by an artist. How close is "Baa, Baa, Black Sheep" to Kipling's life? Does it give a clue to his repeated return to situations that provide the same psychological pattern? Probably, but, for the purpose of examining the stories, the answer is not important. "Baa, Baa, Black Sheep" may constitute either the cause or one more example of Kipling's insight into the minds of characters whose lives become virtually unbearable. There is no doubt that Punch's experience and that of others like him is central to Kipling's understanding of human life. Punch is saved from despair by his mother, but there is no return to the world he knew; his paradise is forever lost.

In these stories of childhood, Anglo-India, and war, the social world is found to be insignificant; other people function as a mere backdrop to the individual soul's struggle to find coherence and integrity. But in certain other stories, many set in Anglo-India, Kipling focuses on the claustrophobic restrictions that can accompany life when the community is too present. In "A Wayside Comedy" (*UD*), the hill town of Kashima is small and enclosed, inhabited by only five Anglo-Indians, Major and Mrs. Vanthuysen, Mr. and Mrs. Boulte, and Captain Kurrell. The other residents are the unnamed, uncounted natives. The story tells of the romantic entanglements that occur when Captain Kurrell transfers his illicit attentions from Mrs. Boulte, who welcomed them, to Mrs. Vanthuysen, who does not. Simultaneously, Mr. Boulte, bored with his wife, turns to Mrs. Vanthuysen, who rejects him as well.

The characters' behavior is accounted for by both the geographical and psychological isolation of their community. Early in the story, the narrator gives his analysis. "All laws weaken in a small and hidden community where there is no public opinion. When a man is absolutely alone in a Station he runs a certain risk of falling into evil ways. This risk is multiplied by every addition to the population up to twelve—the Jury number. After that, fear and consequent restraint begin, and human action becomes less grotesquely jerky."

The dispassionate tone of these lines, almost as if they are describing a scientific experiment in human behavior—put so many people into such an atmosphere and observe what happens—is maintained throughout the tale, intensifying the unpleasant coloring of what is already an unpleasant situation. And Kipling's descriptions heighten this effect. The story's opening line introduces a metaphor. "Fate and the Government of India have turned the Station of Kashima into a prison." But the sentence ends by making Kashima seem even worse, in fact, like hell; "there is no help for the poor souls who are now lying there in torment." Kipling reiterates the comparison to hell; "Kashima was as out of the world as Heaven or the Other Place, and the Dosehri hills kept their secret well." The frequent references to the hills that encircle the town, making it both hill and pit, inescapable, leave no doubt in the reader's mind which "out of the world" place Kashima is more like.

Even after the seductions, attempted or completed, the lies, the humiliating truths, the public disgrace, no one can leave Kashima. The inhabitants are forced to meet each day to take tea, to go tiger shooting, to carry on public conversation. One among them, the Major, knows nothing of what has occurred, and the others' desire to keep him ignorant, to save themselves this last bit of scandal, decrees that they maintain the illusion of congeniality. The rituals of society, which can act neither as a protection nor a neutral space, become instead their punishment. And the chill smile the narrator has maintained throughout this "comedy" is reflected in his parting characterization of "that happy family whose cage was the Dosehri hills."

In a handful of Anglo-Indian stories, Kipling examines the dangers that can derive from attempts to deal within a community with boredom and despair. Adulterous liaisons are a frequent recourse, often seeming more the result of ennui than desire. The narrow confines of Kashima and its paucity of company seem the cause of Captain Kurrell's escapades; we are given no indication that he bears genuine affection toward either woman he pursues. Indeed, he pursues the only two Anglo-Indian women available. One suspects that if there were a third or fourth, Captain Kurrell would move on to them in time. In "The Hill of Illusion" (*UD*), Kipling presents, in dialogue form, the unraveling of a plan for an adulterous elopement. As the woman reveals her intuitive understanding of the sordid demimonde that awaits those who abandon their marriages to run off with others, her lover persists in his rosy view of the future they will share. But the reader, privy to the characters' cynical views of marriage, becomes gradually aware that the woman's estimate of the future is more just than the man's. For we see his impatience and jealousy grow even as he attempts to convince the woman that their life together will be happy. Kipling reveals his characters as caught between the desire to escape the emptiness of the present and the realization that the only answer available to them will lead them into a more sterile, dissatisfied life.

"At the Pit's Mouth" (*UD*) is an even grimmer evocation of an adultery occasioned by boredom and cynicism. The characters are introduced with a fairy-tale formula: "once upon a time there was a Man and his Wife and a Tertium Quid." The line resonates with foreboding, as if the reader is preparing to witness the Fall again. But if the characters' anonymity distances them almost to archetypes, the particularities of the Wife's and Tertium Quid's emotions are developed in their full banality and heartlessness. They treat each other more as a means of amusement than affection and laugh together over the Man's simple letters to the Wife. Because they are afraid that the Man, who is away at his station, will learn of the full extent of their relationship, and because they have never been accepted or protected by the town, they seek out hidden places for their trysts and find their safest spot to be the local cemetery. The story is a small masterpiece of symbolic setting, juxtaposing the social world the characters are fruitlessly trying to escape with the death yard where they meet. The pit comes to represent both the literal grave, which they watch being dug and which the Tertium Quid will come to fill after his death in an accident, and the moral cavity they have dug for themselves. Kipling's title, "At the Pit's Mouth," suggests that these characters stand on the brink of destruction; they could return to safety if they wanted. But they do not. They willingly, if unwittingly, jump headlong into the pit.

"At the Pit's Mouth," like "The Hill of Illusion" and many of Kipling's Anglo-Indian stories, is set in Simla, the Himalayan town to which the English government removed during the hottest Indian months. Relatively cool, geographically protected, Simla became a fashionable place for soldiers on leave, for civil servants on vacation, for wives whose husbands could not leave their stations in the plains. It is often Kipling's setting for tales of courtship, sexual intrigue, and adultery. With a population made up of both a stable group of Anglo-Indians who return each year, who know each other's lives and habits, and a transient group who may appear for a season and never return, Simla provides the location for both long-term, annually renewed liaisons and brief, intense, usually disappointing affairs. Kipling's Simla is worldly and cynical, a place where energetic, witty women have few occupations and bored young men few scruples.

One recurring character in many Simla stories is Mrs. Hauksbee. Attractive, incisive, articulate, with a husband always away at his post, Mrs. Hauksbee spends her time gossiping, capturing young admirers,

15

and on occasion pairing her conquests with appropriate marriageable young women. Introducing her in "Three and—an Extra" (*PTH*), Kipling captures a brittle mixture of intelligence and danger. "She was clever, witty, brilliant, and sparkling beyond most of her kind; but possessed of many devils of malice and mischievousness. She could be nice, though, even to her own sex. But that is another story." Mrs. Hauksbee's energy, while amusing to the reader, finally comes to be seen as her defense against the stultifying atmosphere of this small hill-resort. Surrounded by people from whom she can never escape, she uses her intelligence to manipulate and control. And if she tires of the social ritual and pressure, these elements of Simla life at least give purpose to her days; her glimpse of life without them is even more frightening. In "The Education of Otis Yeere" (*UD*), she imagines her old age, and her voice drops its bantering tone as she moves toward a cool judgment on her life. "No more dances; no more rides; no more luncheons; no more theatricals with supper to follow; no more sparring with one's dearest, dearest friend; no more fencing with an inconvenient man who hasn't wit enough to clothe what he's pleased to call his sentiments in passable speech. . . . No more of anything that is thoroughly wearying, abominable, and detestable, but, all the same, makes life worth the having."

To Mrs. Hauksbee, the pleasures of society give life its value. Social status can define one's self-image; the mask that one assumes for company can demand one's good humor, and the conversational round can approximate comradeship. Mrs. Hauksbee looks on the ambiguous comforts that social life provides and decides that they are preferable to no comforts at all. She takes the merest glimpse into a world stripped of such comforts and illusions and turns gratefully away from the sight. Mrs. Hauksbee and her friends are unique in the Simla stories; to them the consolations of society are real, and they best obtain when one does not examine them too closely. More often, these stories demonstrate Sartre's vision of hell, other people.

But using community as the defining factor is not Kipling's most frequent exploration of psychological terror. More often, it takes the form of a character, a Hummil, Jukes, Punch, or Strangwick, recognizing alone that the universe presents no meaningful order or model for the human being, that, as Elliot L. Gilbert writes, "man is alone in a blank cosmos" (Gilbert, 209), and that the isolation he feels is its only reality.

The Recourse of Work

If some of Kipling's characters confront a vision of themselves or the world outside that frightens or destroys them, a world without moral order or coherence, a few, like Mrs. Hauksbee, embrace a world that defends them from such sights. But many others assume a more purposeful stance toward the fear and despair that seem to be always lurking. They do not succumb, and they do more than avert their eyes; they construct their lives as a rebuke. If the universe does not present a moral order, they will be a part of something that creates its own. It has been lodged as a criticism of Kipling's stories that his characters are not introspective, that they suffer or act but do not probe the sources of their emotions. And some readers blame Kipling himself for not exploring the inner lives of his characters.[7] As we have seen, Kipling can indeed trace the filaments of psychic breakdown. More often, however, he concerns himself with characters who turn their gaze outside themselves, who refuse the vortex of self-absorption by allying themselves with a cause, a duty, a work that is greater than the self. And in his most representative work, Kipling gives the reader a view of what can be gained from choosing the practical over the reflective.

Many of the stories deal with the constructions civilization provides to help men and women defeat their personal demons—political systems, social arrangements, behavioral conventions, moral constraints, daily occupations, networks of acquaintances, all of which give a purpose and rhythm to life. These structures create activities, offer evaluative standards, allow successes, provide comrades. In Kipling's stories, these benefits are highly prized. The stories are often located at the intersection between the public world and the individual consciousness; the choice of a social role is a leap toward power over the self. As one looks at his many stories that deal with people choosing positive action in the face of difficulty, suffering, fear, and chaos, one comes to perceive the salutary value Kipling places on such a choice; he applauds it.

One method that underlies many of Kipling's characters' diverse attempts at sanity, meaning, and fulfillment is that great nineteenth-century solace, work, the endeavor that both occupies and absorbs us, that takes up our energy and binds us to an order larger than ourselves. The capacity for work becomes a mark of character; a devotion to duty more intense than others feel distinguishes admirable human beings. It develops and displays their best qualities, their loyalty to a cause or a task or to others engaged in that task, their perseverance under difficult conditions, their selflessness.

An early tale, "Only a Subaltern" (*UD*), gives a highly idealized portrait of a young second-lieutenant whose commitment to the routine and values of his regiment is so deep-seated that he finally comes, in the eyes of his comrades, to embody the spirit of the service. The dismissive title, which quickly becomes ironic, refers to Bobby Wick, the son of a former commissioner in India, now retired to England. After passing his examination at Sandhurst, the Royal Military College, the young man is posted to a regiment in India. Quickly learning from his commander, Revere, what is expected of him, Bobby soon displays an ability and eagerness that surpass his duty. He has a way with his men, an intuitive understanding and gentle patience. When cholera strikes the regiment, Bobby is called back from leave to tend the sick and dying, to provide comfort, and to boost morale. And his devotion to his men makes him sit by their bedsides for long days and nights, far beyond his military obligations. His unflagging energy is recognized. " 'You're worth half-a-dozen of us, Bobby,' said Revere in a moment of enthusiasm. 'How the devil do you keep it up?' " Worn out from overwork, Bobby eventually contracts cholera himself and dies. He is mourned by all who knew him; his patience, affection, and loyalty have been demonstrated by his punishing hard work. "Only a Subaltern" is a romanticized view of the soldier in India, but Kipling epitomizes in Bobby those qualities he values.

In another early tale, "The Daughter of the Regiment" (*PTH*), Kipling again idealizes, this time in a woman, the moral implications of hard work. The memory of Mrs. McKenna is celebrated by the regiment for which her husband was color-sergeant. Mrs. McKenna's commitment to her husband, her surviving children, and the regiment help her to bear losing five children within fourteen months, all to the illnesses of an Indian climate. And when, in the depths of summer, the regiment is sent upcountry, cholera strikes the men. Mrs. McKenna, like Bobby Wicks, literally works herself to death, this time organizing the other women to bring water to the dying troops. Although she was a huge, red-faced, plain-speaking woman, often a figure of fun to the troops, she is remembered by them with respect and affection. In her self-sacrifice, the narrator declares, she belongs more to the regiment than do the sickly, bewildered raw recruits she nursed. Now, many years later, the narrator has quietly arranged a marriage between the baby Mrs. McKenna left behind when she died and a corporal in the regiment. It was his duty to provide for the girl, the narrator explains. Because of her mother's effort, she too belongs to the regiment. "The Daughter of the Regiment" is a slight tale, but the attitudes toward duty and hard work are clear.

In a later story, "Cold Iron" (*R&F*), Kipling sees the commitment to work as not just the province of the extraordinary human being but the duty of everyone, indeed a mark of humanity itself. The tale is one of many in which Kipling deals with otherworldly creatures. Here, a human infant, abandoned, has been raised by the Fairies. Enjoying the freedom, spontaneity, mystery, and magic of the Fairies' world, the boy yet feels obliquely, like Mowgli in the Jungle Books, the attraction of human life. Kipling uses iron to signify the human world, cold iron, it is called, a metal synonymous with tool-making man, a means of subjugating nature. The boy, at the end of the story, indicates his understanding of his fate, to leave the Fairies and assume a human life, by willingly fastening the iron slave-ring around his neck, a vivid image for the life of work. And the narrator defines the human choice as submission—to one's master and to one's work. To equate human life with slavery is grim and, at times, Kipling does see work as sheer exhausting acquiescence. Moreover, he places the slave-ring against the background of the forest and its warm, playful inhabitants. Still, it is cold iron that endures. The fairyland depicted in the tale is no more; human rationality, perseverance, and hard work have created a new world. And, though the volume in which the story appears, *Rewards and Fairies*, poignantly describes what has been lost, this particular story demonstrates that adult human beings have no other choice; to be fully human is to choose work.

Kipling entitled a volume of stories he published in 1898 *The Day's Work*, and almost every one of these twelve stories deals in some way with the importance and significance of work in people's lives. "The Bridge-Builders" is one of Kipling's most developed treatments of work, here from the viewpoint of the worker and from the divine perspective afforded by the gathering of Hindu gods who discuss human efforts to construct a bridge over the Ganges, the sacred river. The story measures the two realms, the commitment to duty of Findlayson, the chief engineer, and the realm of the gods and their understanding of the fragility of human constructions. First Kipling gives full scope to Findlayson's labors. The story details his knowledge of the bridge, every inch of its metal and brick, whose construction he is supervising; his engineering skill in devising new forms needed for this particular lattice-girder bridge, forms named for him, the Findlayson truss and the Findlayson bolted shoe; his growing comradeship with his assistant Hitchcock; his pride in his work; ultimately, his identification with the bridge. And we see the opposition Findlayson must face, from nature, with its brutal heat, its unmanageable floods, its cholera and smallpox; from inept workmen; from the paucity of money and supplies; and from an ignorant government that thoughtlessly suggests seemingly minor changes only to wipe out months of calculations and effort and demand more months of rethinking and rebuilding. Throughout all this, Findlayson perseveres and, as the story begins, looks forward to the ceremonial opening of the bridge. But his plans are thwarted by the unexpected arrival of heavy rains and flooding. As the river swells its banks, pilings and piers, loose tools and machinery are all swept away. And Findlayson knows that if there is any weakness in the embankments, the bridge will not stand. Finally, caught in the flood, floating down the river, both physically in a loosened boat and mentally in an opium-induced trance, Findlayson slams into a small island, crawls out of his boat to shore and there, half asleep, overhears the conversation of the beast-gods who have gathered with the spirit of the Ganges, Mother Gunga, to weigh the fate of the bridge that they consider an insult to their power and dominion.

The first half of Kipling's story is a vision of the harshness of human labor and its rewards. The success of the bridge and the estimation of his fellow engineers mean everything to Findlayson, "everything that made a hard life worth the living." And the story, in its quotidian detail, makes that hard life real to the reader. But the story's second half takes place in the world of nature and religion, of dream and myth; the gods embody the eternal spirit that endures in the face of man's puny ambition. People die, engineering marvels decay, even new religions arise and fade away; the Hindu gods outlast them all. At this point in the story, the reader may well feel that Findlayson's bridge is doomed. The presence of the gods makes his efforts seem trivial, if not impertinent; the fragility of the bridge seems to call into doubt the value of labor. But the story suggests that the significance of human work can withstand even the perspective of eternity.

For even the gods intuit the power of modern materialism, science, and technology. Krishna arrives, the Well-beloved god, he who represents love and joy, he who is closest to human beings, walks among them, knows their dreams and fears, and knows too their perseverance. Krishna tells the others that their days of power are diminishing, that human knowledge and engineering are creating a new world, one in which men and women make their own plans, use their minds and tools to carry out those plans, a world where they rely less on the gods, indeed, hardly think of them at all. And if the bridge is destroyed, men will raise it anew. Although the gods are loath to believe Krishna, they are uncertain enough to accept the bridge, and allow it to remain standing. The end of the story sees the bridge intact, "not a stone shifted anywhere," and Findlayson and Hitchcock return to work.

In "The Bridge-Builders," Kipling juxtaposes the world of dream with the world of labor, the power of the gods with human self-reliance, nature imbued by the spirit with manufactured materials in service to technology. The story does not deny the power of the first; the flood can destroy, and the gods can choose to frustrate human designs. But it recognizes the emerging power of the second. Human beings at their most committed and hard-working are a match for the gods. In alliance with others of like mind, energy, and commitment, they can create marvels that command the respect of divinity itself. And because the story ends with the world of work, the conversation of the beast-gods seems bracketed by the practical, efficient values of the engineers. The gods are not denied, but they are distanced from us; like Findlayson, we leave them behind and turn our attention to the bridge.

In another tale from *The Day's Work*, this one a fable, Kipling employs a field of horses as speakers for a debate on politics. The American setting makes this story somewhat unusual in Kipling's oeuvre, but the concerns expressed are not. The points raised by the rebellious yellow horse who argues in favor of liberty and equality are answered not by contrary arguments, but by recourse to the nature of work. The way that one works becomes the most powerful indicator of the value of one's ideas.

The horse that preaches freedom defines it as the absence of constraint. And he demonstrates his convictions by throwing from the buckboard any women or children who try to ride him and by falling on any men who try as well. His freedom entails danger and suffering to others. The other horses are profoundly shocked by this behavior; they sympathize with the human victims of the yellow horse's definition of freedom. Moreover, they argue, irresponsible behavior on a horse's part leads to the master's whip, not to liberty. Doing one's work well leads to comfort and reward. But, in these horses' eyes, work is not just for reward; it is an index of character, of maturity. The noble horse is the one who values his own labor and does his best. Devotion to work engenders self-respect and comradeship with coworkers. Being in service to another is not an indignity. The horses who loyally do their job demonstrate a grace and sense of worth that the querulous and fractious yellow horse lacks. Indeed, it would seem that their willing submission to the reins and the welfare of the human beings they serve help create the maturity they demonstrate.

A keen knowledge of one's craft is a quality much admired in Kipling's stories. A narrator will often draw a distinction between the dilettante whose ignorance becomes dangerous and the skilled laborer whose detailed knowledge, drawn from experience, takes on almost a moral quality. A thorough grounding in the intricacies of one's work and a belief in the value of good workmanship become marks of character.

In "'Bread upon the Waters'" (*DW*), the chief engineer, McPhee, leaves his job with one shipping firm because he believes that, as a cost-cutting maneuver, a new and untested board of directors is making demands that will endanger his ship and the men who work on it. To get as much use of the ship as it can, the board requires that its route be completed faster than is wise, and that as little time as possible be spent in dry dock for repairs and maintenance. In addition, the board tries to hide, by frequently and heavily painting the ship, the faults and weaknesses that result from such procedures. McPhee's contempt for such policies has a moral undertone, as if a hidden shoddiness is a species of hypocrisy; "they hid their defeeciencies wi' paint an' cheap gildin'."

McPhee is defined as an honest man who knows the world of merchant ships; "he had a thirty-two years' knowledge of machinery and the humours of ships." He has survived shipwrecks, and his body is scarred with the marks of hard labor. He has been awarded numerous certificates and medals for competence and bravery. As a final sign of his seriousness, the narrator remarks, "he drinks only water while his engines work." McPhee puts his comfort last and his craft first. He and his wife live frugally though respectably, and even her conversation centers on ships. McPhee is the image of the dedicated workman, inevitably bound to clash with such as the new board and the young captain they appoint to McPhee's ship, one who comprehends the conditions under which his employment is taken but agrees to them because he has a young family to support.

After the poorly maintained ship founders in a storm, McPhee's new ship salvages the hulk and its rich cargo. As a reward, McPhee is given a handsome sum of money, enough to retire and live comfortably on. In fact, he and his wife take a long cruise. But even then, his character reasserts itself, and he cannot rest aboard ship. In the story's closing lines, we are told that McPhee left the passengers' cabin, ate with the engineers, and provided them with the benefits of his long, successful experience.

The relationship between money and good work is subtly explored in this story. McPhee, who is willing to leave a good-paying job because he is asked to compromise his performance, is contrasted with the young captain, who participates in a dishonest voyage because he needs the money. And even when he no longer works for pay, McPhee cannot resist entering into the work of a ship; work is his life's blood, not merely his occupation. Kipling believed that the best work is often done for honor. He is not implying that workers should not be rewarded for their labor; one of the reasons McPhee holds the board in contempt is that it scrimps by feeding the crew badly. To care as best one can for one's subordinates redounds to the honor of owners and masters. But the good worker's loyalty is not meted out to fit the monetary reward; it is given freely by love of the work itself. And in fact many of the workers Kipling celebrates in his stories are those whose salary is meager, nonexistent, or inconsequential. Mrs. McKenna labors to bring water to the dying men out of love and duty. And Findlayson wants only the esteem of those who know how to estimate good bridges.

It is the union of McPhee's detailed knowledge and his commitment to the good of the ship that makes him admirable in Kipling's view. Meticulous expertise in service to a noble cause constitutes, in many of Kipling's stories, the highest kind of life. So enthusiastic can Kipling be about the minutiae of a craft that such knowledge can be the standard by which acquaintances become friends. In "The Disturber of Traffic" (*MI*), the frame narrator meets Fenwick, a lighthouse keeper who knows all there is to know about navigation. It is only when the narrator demonstrates sufficient information to earn Fenwick's respect, information derived not from mere hearsay but experience, that the two can converse as equals. "Hereupon he ceased to talk down to me, and became so amazingly technical that I was forced to beg him to explain every other sentence. This set him fully at his ease; and then we spoke as men together, each too interested to think of anything except the subject in hand."

In fact, Kipling's love of technical language has resulted in some tales being overweighted with jargon, as if plot, character, and atmosphere were all mere devices to justify paragraphs of shop talk. Kipling had a love of navigational language and a sound grasp of ship construction, for example. These two mingle in a large group of tales written during his middle years, often in the narrator's dialect, that are virtually clotted with insider's knowledge: "The Disturber of Traffic," "The Ship that Found Herself" (*DW*), "The Devil and the Deep Sea" (*DW*), "The Bonds of Discipline" (*T&D*), " 'Their Lawful Occasions' " (*T&D*). Even at the end of his career, he returned to this love of the seafarer's language in "Sea Constables" (*D&C*). And his enjoyment of the intricate language of the professional extended to arenas as diverse as polo—"The Maltese Cat" (*DW*) is told from the point of view of the horses—and the world of trains—"—007" (*DW*) is spoken by both the train engineers and the trains themselves, all in the argot of the roundhouse. His stories of soldiers, moreover, those in India, in South Africa, on the front in World War I, all give the details and slang of the infantryman's life. At times the technical language of the tales can impede narrative, creating an almost obsessive style, but all these stories reveal Kipling's respect for the individual whose detailed practical knowledge is based on experience, not theory.

Kipling wrote many tales about the world of medicine, of scientists, technicians, chemists, researchers, and, particularly, physicians. In these stories, he is able to deal with the rational, practical temperament allied to the purposeful, selfless character, a nexus where knowledge, imagination, and faith join to promote healing. Although he wrote a few stories about doctors early in his career, the subject grows in importance in the later stories. It is especially prevalent in *Rewards and Fairies*, a collection that deals with many kinds of healing. In "A Doctor of Medicine" (*R&F*), for example, the seventeenth-century astrologer and physician Nicholas Culpepper is presented as one who, following a now-discredited theory of the influence of the stars on illness and health, discovers the relationship between the plague and the rats that transmit it. Culpepper summarizes the scope of knowledge and the philosophical composure necessary to the healer. " 'I myself,' said he, 'have saved men's lives, and not a few neither, by observing at the proper time—there is a time, mark you, for all things under the sun—by observing, I say, so small a beast as a rat in conjunction with so great a matter as this dread arch above us.' He swept his hand across the sky."

Culpepper is presented within the imaginative frame of *Rewards and Fairies;* the young children of the present day, Dan and Una, have conjured up for them visions of earlier men and women who walked the Sussex ground they now tread. Culpepper is one of their visitors, and his outmoded amalgamation of science and pseudoscience at first brings a smile to the children and, perhaps, to the reader. But his devotion to those who are ill, epitomized by his willingness to attend a town stricken by the plague despite warnings to stay away, wins his listeners' respect.

So too does his honest recognition that his long-held herbal remedies do not suffice against this dread disease. He bravely enters an infected dwelling to observe and wait for guidance from the stars. Culpepper decides that the plague is the result of a long-standing battle between the Moon and Mars, and that the dying rats, the representatives of the Moon, are being overcome by the influence of Mars. He allies himself with Mars, and, winning the assistance of the villagers, seeks out, kills, and burns the rats, halting the spread of the plague.

The reader knows, though Culpepper does not, that the true cause of disease is germs, not celestial animosities. Kipling cloaks Culpepper's heroism in a light irony. And he often treats his physicians in this manner, as if acknowledging that reason is fallible, that good intentions are not enough, that what seems like proven science today may turn out to be delusion tomorrow. But the moral and intellectual qualities Culpepper displays, devotion to the sick even to the point of personal danger; fidelity to the facts born of observation, hypothesis, and experiment; willingness to take the risk of the imaginative solution when the long-held ones fail; perseverance when one's answers are unpopular, and a capacity for hard, unremitting labor, all these characterize, for Kipling, quintessential medicine. Kipling's doctors are not always successful. Like Spurstow in "At the End of the Passage," the enemy they fight may be too strong for science and compassion. But Kipling often treats the doctor as a soldier in a noble cause.

His medical practitioners often demonstrate the combination of hard work and imagination which, to Kipling, is the height of fruitful labor. Hard work is not equated with mindless toil. It may come to that, and in their capacity to endure, Sisyphus-like, in an unending endeavor, human beings may demonstrate nobility, even heroism. Likewise, submerging private grief in the daily rounds of an occupation may make life bearable for a while, but Kipling generally puts a different emphasis on the salutary nature of work. Like Carlyle, whom he so much resembles in his understanding of the spiritual implications of work,[8] Kipling believes that human beings can perfect themselves in their work. The demands of a complex, problem-filled duty can call forth the full resources of our intellect and imagination. In studying a problem, locating its source, hypothesizing a solution, developing and then implementing a means of putting that solution into practice, perhaps succeeding or perhaps failing, and then resuming the procedure from the beginning, we draw forth our best mental and moral qualities, indeed develop and refine those qualities.

It is imagination, for example, that distinguishes Kipling's most admired doctors. It is Culpepper's receptivity to his observations and his ability to correlate those with his astral philosophy that lead him to drive out and destroy the rats. In "Marklake Witches" (*R&F*), another tale in which Dan and Una encounter a character from the past, they learn of the work of Rene, a French prisoner of war, in fact, Dr. Rene Laennec, the inventor of the stethoscope. Laennec's "trumpet," by which he can hear the sounds in people's chests, makes him a source of amusement and fear to the English peasants. But Laennec battles their ignorance in an effort to diagnose a young girl dying of tuberculosis. Though unable to cure her, he yet represents the force of intelligence and science allied with imagination and compassion.

So too in "The Tender Achilles," Wilkett, the young medical researcher whose mind has been broken by practicing often-futile surgery at the battlefront, is valued by his professional colleagues not merely for his single-minded devotion. " 'He has got imagination,' Sir Thomas pointed out. 'That's what his coming back to St. Peggotty's will give the whole team.' "

And in one of his last stories, "Unprofessional" (*L&R*), Kipling develops in rich detail many of the qualities he associates with medicine, its combination of meticulous attention to material detail with the need for imagination, its union of intellectual prowess and the moral urge to help others, its desire to manipulate nature and its helplessness in the face of intractable fate, its ability to cheat death but only temporarily, and its tendency to create close bonds of fellowship among its practitioners. The story tells of four old friends who, when one, Harries, inherits a large sum of money, are freed from the demands of earning a living and allowed to pursue what most interests them. Two have been doctors tied to a practice they detest. One, Vaughan, sets up the nursing home he had always dreamed of; the second, Loftie, embarks on medical research. Harries pursues his old interest in astrology, and the fourth, Ackerman, acts as a general manager and liaison for the entire project. As the story develops, the interests of the three scientists converge; they observe the influence of planetary motion on laboratory experiments and use their knowledge to benefit the residents of the nursing home. Kipling portrays their total absorption in their work, freely chosen without regard for pay. Work is the calling one pursues when one is relieved of wordly cares; it reconciles one to oneself, and connects one to the lives of others who benefit from the labor. In this tale, as in "A Doctor of Medicine," Kipling associates medicine with astrology, but here the connection is not viewed as a remnant of an outworn philosophy. Astrology here does predict the movement of cells; following the astrological clues does result in determining the most propitious time for medical intervention in illness. Astrology becomes a suggestive, mysterious subject for science to explore, a representative of what is yet unknown by rational man.

Absorption in work, then—its detail and lore, the public good that derives from it, the friendships it brings—can provide a goal and daily occupation for human beings. It can help develop and sustain qualities of character that might have been left dormant. It can contribute to psychic health. Many of Kipling's characters are alone in a blank universe, without any support beyond their own constructions and efforts; work becomes their sustenance, direction, comfort, and reward.

The Idea of Empire

In many ways, Kipling's work can be seen as a dialogue between characters who embrace the vivifying power of action and those who retreat to a dreamy, anarchic, destructive solitude. Those who choose action may do so for a wide spectrum of reasons, from a desperate need for some support beyond the foundering self to a belief in the inherent value of a specific cause. Often those motives are inextricably intertwined.

But the movement beyond the self to work and community is a persistent, positive motif in Kipling's stories. And Kipling investigates many different communities devoted to an ethos and to hard, demanding work, the soldier's life, professional societies, the navy, groups of men involved in a single task. But the community with which he is most popularly identified is the Anglo-Indian, and the task is Empire building. Kipling has been criticized for being the laureate of a politically ruthless, self-aggrandizing, racist, exploitive endeavor, the apologist of a movement now discredited.[9] Indeed, the fall in his literary reputation can be attributed, to a great extent, to his association with the Raj. Even within Kipling's lifetime, public support for the English presence in India wavered. And as more recent writers have made vivid the human cost of imperialism, the economic, political, and social exploitation, the infantalizing of native populations—not only in India but in central Africa, South Africa, southeast Asia, the Caribbean, Latin America, in well-known and obscure parts of the globe—it has become increasingly difficult to enter with any sympathy into the minds of those who seem to support the imperial project.

As will become apparent, one can easily find in Kipling's stories examples of the repugnant behavior of those in colonial power. Although many of the Anglo-Indian stories employ a complex narrative line and an ironic tone that make it difficult to determine exactly where their author's sympathies lie, many present a seemingly straightforward defense of imperialism. But reading these latter tales in light of Kipling's ideas about social community and the relationship between public work and private psyche can help extricate them from conventional patterns of interpretation and put Kipling's attitude toward imperialism in a larger and perhaps juster perspective.

Kipling began writing about India when he returned there in 1882, at the age of sixteen, to work as assistant editor of the *Civil and Military Gazette*. He wrote sketches, reports, reviews, and, in general, anything needed to fill the newspaper's pages. But in 1886, under a new editor, he began writing "turnovers," stories that started on the front page and continued on the second. These stories, brief, written hastily for a newspaper's readership, nevertheless provided a remarkable indication of Kipling's great talent and broad, if still growing, knowledge of Indian life, from the hill station of Simla to the opium dens of Lahore, from the tedious routine of civil servants to the toughening days of soldiers. In 1887, Kipling was sent to Allahabad to write for the larger, more prestigious *Pioneer*. The stories from this period, released from the space limitations of "turnovers," are somewhat longer and more leisurely, though still relatively short and tightly constructed as befits fiction written for a newspaper. It was not until he returned to England that Kipling developed his Indian material in its fullest and richest style.

The exigencies of journalism as well as the immediacy of living in India, surrounded by the very people and events informing his fiction, combine to make the earliest stories brief and anecdotal, snapshots of Anglo-Indian life taken under a bright light with few shadows. In "The Rescue of Pluffles" (*PTH*), for example, the narrator turns to Mrs. Hauksbee and her set. Pluffles, a callow subaltern, has fallen impetuously in love with the older, experienced Mrs. Riever, who leads him to squander his money on gifts for her, perform ignominious errands on her behalf, and, in general, demean himself and provide a source of amusement for all Simla onlookers. Mrs. Hauksbee, knowing that Pluffles's English fiancée is coming out to India for the marriage, decides simultaneously to save Pluffles from his own folly and to humiliate Mrs. Riever, an old rival.

The story ends with Pluffles safely wed and returned to England. The narrator comments approvingly on his fate: "he would have come to extreme grief in India." The story is slight and no character is explored, though the superiority of women in dealing with social practicalities is suggested, an opinion often expressed in the worldly Simla stories. "The Rescue of Pluffles" is simply another episode in the daily life that makes up this brittle, enclosed society, the fringe of the Empire.

In "Venus Annodomini" (*PTH*), Kipling treats another sophisticated, beautiful woman and another escape of a young devotee. Here the age of the unnamed woman, left purposely vague but slyly suggested, is of major importance; "she was as immutable as the Hills. But not quite so green." The charming and clever woman finds among her admirers "Very Young Gayerson," who promptly makes a fool of himself in his abject devotion to her and, moreover, does nothing to conceal his folly. It is only when Very Young Gayerson discovers first, that the woman's daughter is indeed older than he, and second, that his own father had once been the woman's suitor, that he decides to leave Simla. The tone of both these stories is jocular and knowing, told as if the worldly narrator were winking at us, inviting us into a circle where the wealthy and idle elbow for social position and the innocent and easily duped become fodder for dinner-table repartee. But Kipling's narrator is not entirely a member of the dominant social group; he is enough of an insider to know its manners and values, but stands sufficiently outside to mark its hollowness. This ambivalent stance, amused yet faintly repelled, characterizes many of the Simla stories.

So too in treating the soldiers in India, Kipling often maintains a distance from his subjects. In "The Three Musketeers" (*PTH*), he introduces Mulvaney, Ortheris, and Learoyd, three Anglo-Indian privates who will become major representatives of the common soldier facing the rigors of military life, the isolation of the foreigner in a strange land, and the harshness of the Indian climate. The narrator sympathizes with the three men, who recount the hoax they devised against a visiting British nobleman who created a nuisance by making imperious demands. By surreptitiously kidnapping and then publicly rescuing their victim, they had become heroes, the nobleman had been hospitalized from fright, and all problems had been solved. Again, Kipling's narrative stance is more complex than might at first appear.

He elicits sympathy for the soldiers by pitting them against an easy butt, the ignorant and pompous civilian from abroad. But he draws a clear distinction between himself and his three soldiers. His framing narrative and explanatory passages are given in standard English; his soldiers speak in heavy dialect. As we learn in other stories, Mulvaney is an Irishman, Ortheris a Cockney, and Learoyd a Yorkshireman. Kipling attempts to reproduce these accents, telling the story in an at times almost impenetrable cacophony of sounds. We the readers are as hard put as the narrator to understand the language of these men. We can sympathize with them, yet know that they do not represent us. Not only is their language too foreign, their hoax is too crude and harsh to be fully justified. They are uneducated and coarse. Although Kipling's narrator professes affection for them whenever they appear, an affection we come to some extent to share, these three soldiers always remain somewhat removed from us in expression and sensibility.

Watching Kipling control the distance between the reader and the characters in these early Indian stories is one of the pleasures in studying them. As brief, and at times as almost artless as they seem, they yet repay close attention to structure and tone. They possess an ambivalence, a mixture of sympathy and astringency, that gives them a unique and instantly recognizable perspective.

In "A Bank Fraud" (*PTH*), Kipling contrasts a character whose body and spirit are unequal to India with another who has learned to negotiate the difficult passages presented. Reggie Burke, the manager of a local branch of a Calcutta-based bank, has been saddled with a new accountant, ignorant of India, arrogant about his banking experience, which, it turns out, has been in a few provincial Yorkshire towns. The accountant, Riley, is, moreover, dying of consumption, though he does not know it. Riley spends his time criticizing and badgering Burke about his poor business sense and immoral friends. But Burke, knowing of Riley's illness, stays on to nurse him. In addition, he perpetrates a series of "frauds" on the dying boy. Riley has been fired by the bank's directors; not only does Burke keep this knowledge from him, he forges official commendatory letters to Riley. He pays Riley's salary out of his own pocket, and sends more money to the boy's mother. His aim is to keep Riley alive, keep his spirits up. When finally all maneuvers fail, as they must, and Riley dies, Burke feels only sadness that he could not keep him alive for another day.

The story pits two personalities, two responses to hardship, against each other. Burke is tolerant and flexible; he is an efficient manager but also has a wide circle of friends, enjoys dances, and plays polo. He has made a tolerable life for himself in India. But Riley, new to the country, lacks the ability to move beyond those narrow standards devised in a foreign land and now totally inadequate. The narrator remarks, "he was useless for Upper India and a wheat Province, where a man wants a large head and a touch of imagination." Kipling's stories often comment on the disparity between English expectations and Indian reality; the values and habits born in a small country, with a homogeneous population, established religious beliefs, and orthodox public standards of morality cannot be uncompromisingly retained in a complex culture of heterodox races, traditions, and values, where the dominant political power barely understands the great masses it rules, and the masses tend to slip quietly out of the bonds imposed on them to go their own way. The vitality and mystery of Indian culture together with its unyielding climate make tolerance necessary. As the narrator comments in "Thrown Away," "India is a place beyond all others where one must not take things too seriously—the mid-day sun always excepted."

But the mark of Reggie Burke's "imagination" is his desire to care for an unpleasant young man, to reach out beyond his own self-interest to comfort another. Such protectiveness, mixed in some stories with a rueful wit, occurs in many of the Indian tales, as if these characters, in their geographical isolation, found their human bonds to be a necessary recourse. Friendship, even discordant at times, makes Anglo-Indian life more bearable. But Reggie Burke's motives remain somewhat mysterious; he never develops an affection for Riley, and it seems almost as if the challenge of keeping Riley alive helps keep Reggie going as well. Again we are left outside a situation, distanced from the protagonist, not quite sure how the narrator interprets the tale.

Though Kipling left India in 1889, at the age of twenty-three, he continued to write about the land and its inhabitants for many years. The stories become a more elaborate exploration of the Empire and its meaning. Longer, often more panoramic in geography, the later stories are simultaneously more idealized and more searching about the role of the Anglo-Indian. Characters tend to be less psychologically developed and more representative of what Kipling sees as the complex condition of the Empire. Imperialism itself becomes less a political cause and more an artistic construct, less a perceived reality and more an idea. Though from his earliest stories Kipling seems more interested in the English people who went out to India than the justice of the cause that sent them, in his later Indian tales, he looks at the imperial adventure as the experience of work that did public good and gave private satisfaction; it is imperialism as daily labor in the service of an immediate practical end, bridge building or sanitation, that comes to symbolize its value. That is not to say that Kipling does not see the costs, both to the colonizer and the colonized, but if he is a spokesman for imperialism, it is, to use Elliott Gilbert's phrase, for imperialism as metaphor.[10]

In "The Tomb of his Ancestors" (*DW*), Kipling presents the relationship between one Anglo-Indian family, the Chinns, and the ancient, wild Indian race of Bhils. Chinn men have traveled out to India for generations, and the Bhils, the group they traditionally supervised, have come to love them. Indeed, the first Chinn has been elevated in Bhil legend to the status of a god, with a tomb that is decorated and venerated. The newest Chinn in returning to the land of his birth is instantly recognized by the Bhils and accorded the love his name has earned. In fact, the story is an account of the mutual love and loyalty that obtain between a selfless, paternalistic Englishman and a savage but childlike people. They protect each other. The Bhils teach young John Chinn to survive in the wilderness; he persuades them to be vaccinated against the rampant smallpox and kills the tiger that has been terrorizing their community.

When a child, John Chinn had been sent back to England to be educated. As the story opens, he is returning to Central India. He quickly begins speaking a few words in the Bhil language, although he did not realize he still remembered it. He is sought out by the Bhils, who insist on acting as his servants and teachers. Throughout the story, John Chinn is seen as a father to the Bhils, but they nourish and defend each other. Chinn's life is one moment in a long history of mutual sustenance; the Bhils remark that they are anticipating Chinn's marriage and the birth of a new son to be part of his life. Chinn himself sees his place in the family and the cause it serves; "Yes; it's a big work—all of it—even my little share." It is a work that brings few public rewards but improves the lives of people. The narrator remarks of Chinn's grandfather, who protected the Bhils, taught them to plow and to sow, learned their language, and lived among them, "it was slow, unseen work, of the sort that is being done all over India today; and though John Chinn's only reward came, as I have said, in the shape of a grave at Government expense, the little people of the hills never forgot him."

Kipling looks at the undeveloped, seemingly ungovernable country that is India and defines imperialism in these stories as a work to be done, a civilizing, humane work, with few rewards but a sense of accomplished good. One of his fullest treatments of this view is in "William the Conqueror," which like "The Tomb of his Ancestors" is included in *The Day's Work*. Unlike the earlier anecdotal tales, this story has a

33

large geographical sweep, from the social life of an Anglo-Indian town in the northern district of Lahore with its Club and Mall, along the Indian Desert, to the dry, dusty, brutally hot South. It takes place during a famine, when Martyn, a police official, and Scott, an irrigation engineer, are pressed into serving in famine relief. Martyn's sister, William, accompanies her brother to the South, and the story recounts Scott's and William's individual work to provide food for those in the famine camps.

Scott and Martyn are members of the lower branches of the civil service; their poverty and frugality are stressed. Moreover, there is no career advancement in their famine work; they are uprooted from their normal work, and Scott, in particular, loses the opportunity to pursue the job he likes best. But they and William plunge willingly into their work. Scott must travel, by foot and cart, long stretches of the Indian countryside, feeding and transporting the starving. His exhausting labors are detailed: sleeping by day under his cart, traveling by night when it is cool, learning to milk goats to feed dying babies, distributing his few supplies to the skeletal and desperate poor who clamor for food, devising ways to use grain to feed those who will eat only rice, writing reports, repairing his carts, keeping an eye out for possible sites for irrigation devices. And, coming to the end of one trip, he must turn back and, without rest, begin again. Finally, ill with fever and exhaustion, he collapses. By then, however, the worst of the famine is over; the rains have come.

The story is told in harsh vignettes of a desperate landscape, women selling their children for food, or giving them up to the government in the hope the babies will at least be fed, corpses littering the road as the famine trains go by, old railroad cars used for burning the dead, the emaciated everywhere. This is Indian life when geography and climate are at their worst. And the response of the English government may be clumsy—too many telegrams and contradictory orders—but the men and women who serve the government are seen as heroic. They leave behind all thoughts of self to give practical aid, secure good water, feed the hungry, give medicine to the ill; they spend their own meager money to buy milk and repair carts.

Scott, on the road, and William, in the famine camp, represent Kipling's concept of work at its highest: efficient, imaginative, energetic, self-effacing, persevering. And it is the Empire that puts these qualities at the disposal of those in great need. Kipling's ideal of Empire is the setting aside of personal desire to be part of a cause of practical benefit to those in a teeming, brutal, chaotic land. Government makes this effort possible; it creates the systems, political, economic, civil, that make places for such as Scott and William. Empire in "William the Conqueror" has nothing to do with political annexation. It is service. It provides an arena where moral fiber can be put to work. As in "The Bridge-Builders," the hard practical effort to bring improvement becomes the paramount concern. Political causes are very far away, usually irrelevant, often inhibitory.

In his study of Kipling's concept of law, Shamsul Islam argues that Kipling's view of imperialism cannot be equated with the British Raj; rather, it is an ideal of order and good. "Kipling's concept of Empire is a much deeper concept than is generally recognized. Essentially Empire stands for the forces of law, order and discipline which are engaged in a constant struggle against the negative forces of chaos, confusion and disorder. So Kipling's imperial drama assumes the proportions of a morality play in a non-theological sense."[11]

"William the Conqueror" and "The Tomb of his Ancestors" show the Empire at its best, but they are heavily idealized, indeed mythic, stories. John Chinn's grandfather has become a deity to the Bhils, and they believe that divinity breathes through the young Chinn as well. The young man, intuiting his great power, uses it only benevolently. He is successful in all he attempts, and his efforts are greeted enthusiastically by his fellow Englishmen. And Scott, in "William the Conqueror," though exhausted by work, accomplishes great good and is loved by all who meet him. So idealized is Scott, he appears at one point as a god. He returns to the base camp after a long trip distributing famine relief, surrounded by the goats he has kept and the babies he has collected and fed. "He had no desire to make any dramatic entry, but an accident of the sunset ordered it that, when he had taken off his helmet to get the evening breeze, the low light should fall across his forehead, and he could not see what was before him; while one waiting at the tent door beheld, with new eyes, a young man, beautiful as Paris, a god in a halo of golden dust, walking slowly at the head of his flocks, while at his knee ran small naked Cupids." This is William's epiphany, the moment she falls in love with Scott. But we readers by this time see him through a romantic haze as well. Scott and John Chinn have ceased to exist in the same terms as Mrs. Hauksbee or Hummil. They have been exalted, apotheosized as the Empire.

These stories display Kipling's ideal of Empire, and Scott and John Chinn, like Findlayson, represent faithful labor in noble service. But, writing largely without narrative irony, Kipling does not see the implications of his own language, the paternalism that defines Indians as perpetual children, the authoritarianism that assumes the Englishman's right to decide the fate of natives, the tone of physical and moral usurpation that pervades the treatment of imperialism. Still, Kipling is never a simple apologist for the political and social realities of the Empire. Particularly in the early stories, but even in the later, he demonstrates a sharp perception of the sacrifices demanded by service in an imperialistic cause in a harsh land, distant from those who make the decisions. In "William the Conqueror," Scott's physical suffering is made clear. We have already examined, in "At the End of the Passage" and "The Strange Ride of Morrowbie Jukes," the loneliness, alienation, and despair that can accompany life as a colonizing power. Kipling pays a great deal of attention to the effects of the Empire on the imperialists themselves. And the very recourse that he often urges in times of difficulty, work, can, in India, destroy rather than help.

Kipling has a number of stories about the deleterious effects of overwork. "In the Pride of His Youth" (*PTH*) traces the young life of Dicky Hatt, a poor English boy who looks forward to his service in India as a way to improve his prospects. Dicky marries secretly before he leaves England, but he cannot afford to bring his wife to the East. Forced to support himself and her, and later their son, he lives in miserable poverty, refusing to squander money on any amusements, working at a crushing pace. Finally his wife, disappointed at not being able to join him, in despair over the death of their child, leaves him for another man. Dicky abandons his mind-numbing, exhausting job, never to return. Work in this tale is not salutary; it does not develop moral qualities or contribute to the welfare of others. It drains strength and defeats hope. Poverty is not a romanticized making-do; it destroys. And Kipling has many stories of minor civil servants who, though mere cogs in the machinery of the Empire, are driven past endurance.

But many of Kipling's imperial characters suffer the effects of their government's treatment, even if not in such a dramatic manner as Dicky Hatt. The civil service and the military, two substructures that support the Empire by demanding sacrifice but offering security, both produce lives curiously truncated or warped. In "The Courting of Dinah Shadd" (*LH*), we learn of Mulvaney's youth and marriage. And although he has wed an exemplary woman he deeply loves, we see a strange, self-destructive streak in his character, one responsible for a lifetime of hardship for him and his Dinah.

In "The Madness of Private Ortheris," we have seen a homesickness so profound it almost leads to desertion. And numerous other tales of Kipling's soldiers recount a gruffness, a crudeness that interferes with a normal life. These professional soldiers, often far away from those they love, thrown upon each other for support, inured to harsh discipline, meting out a brutal death to their country's enemies, seem perpetually caught between childishness and cynicism. In "His Private Honour" (*MI*), the rigor of military training is detailed; unrelieved work and strict, at times irrational, discipline are needed to turn recruits into soldiers. Drill and insults breed comradeship and obedience to superiors. It is only in suffering together that men forge the bonds necessary to success in battle. The men emerge, however, not simply hardened, but calloused.

Indeed, Kipling's stories of men and women who do the work of the Empire often raise serious questions about the moral effects such work has on those who perform it. The need for internal order, which might be satisfied by conforming one's character to an external order, can pass over into the need to control others, into brutality and cynicism. Kipling has many stories that portray hoaxes; in those that treat his youthful schooldays, the tales of *Stalky & Co.*, the sympathy is usually with the prankster, as if the narrator unambiguously embraces the adolescent's desire for power and urge to humiliate others. These stories have dismayed some of Kipling's readers, though others to be sure find them an enthusiastic portrayal of schoolboy highjinks. But, in his Indian tales about hoaxes, Kipling's narrative stance is cooler, as if the joke being played might be too harsh or might be played on the wrong person.

In "The Rout of the White Hussars" (*PTH*), an overbearing colonel demands the selling of the regiment's drum horse, a noble animal of which the men are proud. Two of the subalterns pretend to kill the horse and then, when the regiment is in battle, send it back with a skeleton astride. The terrified troops retreat in panic, and the regiment and its colonel are humiliated. The colonel, to save everyone's reputation, agrees to keep the entire episode a secret. It is difficult to see exactly who is being punished in the story. The regiment's reputation is threatened, though the men opposed the sale of the horse. The colonel, at first embarrassed by the prank, discovers that in protecting his troops' reputation, he has enhanced his own among them.

The two pranksters are safe. No one is hurt. And the entire episode seems the plot of the childish against the mean-spirited. All the characters emerge as unpleasant.

So too the tone of "The Arrest of Lieutenant Golightly" (*PTH*) is harsh and unsympathetic. Golightly, who prides himself on his appearance, is caught in a downpour while returning to his duties from a leave. The story follows his comical misadventures. His drenched uniform is streaked by the bad dyes, his horse falls lame, and he is forced to walk. In this shabby state, he is mistaken for a deserter and arrested. Golightly is saved only when recognized by one of his superiors. But his humiliating story is spread among the soldiers, and the once-proud Golightly is humbled. The story does not sympathize with Golightly; rather, the vain lieutenant seems to get what he deserved. The perspective is that of Golightly's fellow soldiers, amused at his comeuppance. These soldiers find their pleasure in laughing at each other.

In the frame to "The Drums of the Fore and Aft" (*WWW*), the narrator investigates at some length the nature of army life and the kinds of harsh discipline that must be imposed on men if they are to perform brutal duty. These soldiers are ill-educated young boys, sent out to India ignorant of the country and their role in it. They are part of an army often involved in mortal skirmishes, often suspecting they are expendable. It is no wonder, the narrator remarks, that they are unreliable until fully broken in by training, until they cease to think for themselves and come to resemble reliable machines. For their job, as the narrator sums it up, is "to do butcher's work with efficiency and despatch." Kipling had a clear view of what constituted army life, of what soldiers became. If he romanticizes the Anglo-Indian soldier at times, he also portrays the cost to man's humanity when he assumes his military role.

And he sees the limitations of fatuous government officials who do not know what they are demanding. In "Tods' Amendment" (*PTH*), he treats the passage of a bill that will affect hundreds of thousands of Indian tenant farmers. In theory, one provision of the bill seemed sensible: to protect the farmer from oppressive landlords, it demanded that no land be leased for more than five years. But, officials, both Indian and Anglo-Indian, who have devised the bill have no understanding of the native Punjabis' customs and fears; such an impermanent tenancy would cause hardship and dislocation. The narrative is told with biting contempt for the ignorant administrators. "The Native

Member of Council knew as much about Punjabis as he knew about Charing Cross. . . . The Legal Member's knowledge of natives was limited to English-speaking Durbaris, and his own red *chaprassis*." The narrator concludes, "no man can tell what natives think unless he mixes with them with the varnish off. And not always then." For these are government representatives who do not know the language, the values, or the traditions of the people they govern. No matter how honorable their intentions, they are bound to make serious mistakes.

Tods, the Anglo-Indian child who knows Urdu, who chats with his nurse in her native tongue, who seeks out shopkeepers and coolies for friends, becomes the emissary for the natives by repeating to the officials the reservations the farmers have about the new system. Tods lives in two worlds; he calls the natives "brother," knows their language and thoughts, and is yet an Anglo-Indian, part of the world of the Empire. But Tods will lose his privileged status; his mother, fearing he is becoming too close to the Indians, plans to send him back to England for his education. If he does return, he will be thoroughly Anglicized, one more member of the Empire out of touch with the natives he governs.

Kipling's stories of Anglo-India reveal a profound understanding of the instability of the English position. One of Kipling's most famous tales, "The Man Who Would Be King" (*PR*), embodies imperial pretensions in shifting lights. This rich story is virtually a farrago of imperial ideas, some presented sympathetically, some in parody, and some in tones too complex and unsteady to be labeled simply.[12] The exploits of Peachey Taliaferro Carnehan and Daniel Dravot, two ne'er-do-well, itinerant adventurers, are presented to us through an intermediary, an unnamed narrator; although a narrative frame is a favorite device of Kipling, it functions here in particularly complicated ways. The narrator, an Anglo-Indian newspaperman, is drawn into Peachey and Dan's story by agreeing to deliver a message from one to the other. He is later pressed to help them plan their adventure by supplying encyclopedias and maps of the area they wish to explore. Finally, he is the audience to whom the survivor, Peachey, tells his tale. Both a marginal accomplice and an objective listener, drawn in sympathy by the energy and daring of the men's vision, but repelled by its audacity and foregone failure, the narrator hears, witnesses, participates in, and comments on the story he tells us.

That story recounts Peachey and Dan's excursion into Kafiristan, unexplored territory in northern Afghanistan, of their desire to establish themselves as kings, to conquer and rule the natives, to accumulate wealth and power. And they accomplish all their aims. By arming and training small groups of natives who then form their defense against the rest of the population, by establishing their own authority and putting an end to petty tribal wars, by drawing on the Masonic traditions they and the natives know, by using their wits to impress the credulous primitive people, they become rulers in Kafiristan; Dan Dravot indeed becomes a king.

Peachey and Dan, while ambitious and daring, are themselves astonished at their success. They subjugate the natives through military might and political annexation, but they solidify their victory when they discover that their subjects know Masonic lore. The adventurers use their superior knowledge and the respect it brings them to win permanent obeisance. They have learned that true power is held not merely by guns but by using the culture of the powerless to support one's regime. " 'Peachey,' says Dravot, 'we don't want to fight no more. The Craft's the trick, so help me!' " and Dravot's ambitions grow. " 'I won't make a Nation,' says he. 'I'll make an Empire!' "

Peachey and Dan become simultaneously representatives and parodies of the Empire builders Kipling elsewhere idealizes. They employ the methods of the imperialist—military, political, cultural—but do so only for personal aggrandizement. Peachey and Dan represent an attempt at Empire without the moral values that, to Kipling, validate that attempt. They lack commitment to the native population, to standards of justice, to honor. And the story reveals the fate of imperial designs without a moral center: Peachey and Dan are attacked by their troops; Dan is killed, Peachey tortured and released to die.

But Kipling's story resists an easy condemnation of Peachey and Dan. They are, in many ways, sympathetic characters. Energetic, bold, imaginative, with a sense of humor and a delight in their own talent, they win the reader's interest and assent, even as they forfeit approval. And they are faithful to each other. Knowing he will be killed, Dan urges Peachey to flee, but Peachey responds, "Go to Hell, Dan! I'm with you here." Because they are not so much villains as rogues, they never fully embody the dark side of imperialism. Moreover, Kipling's complex narrative frame prevents our dismissing Peachey and Dan. The narrator's ambivalent response becomes ours, and, when Peachey returns to tell his tale, the vivid evidence of his intense suffering—his physical scars and mental fragility, his moving in and out of sane discourse—creates an affecting portrait. "The Man Who

Would Be King" is one of Kipling's most analyzed stories; there is no doubt it contains a searching exploration of the dangers of imperial ambition, but it hedges that investigation by implicating the narrator and the reader. We sympathize with the adventurers while we see their exploitation of others. Again, as so often in his portraits of the Empire, Kipling creates a complex, distanced story whose ultimate attitude toward the events it depicts remains somewhat mysterious.

Peachey and Dan look on the natives of Kafiristan as simply people to be subdued in order to promote their own authority. And if Kipling investigates the effects of imperialism on the imperialist, his attitude toward the native Indian population, as it operates in his fiction, is the second crucial aspect of his conception of imperialism that must be considered. There is no doubt that mixed with the good imperial England thought it was doing in India was a profound assumption that the Indians were a more primitive people, unwilling or unable to govern themselves, a teeming populace of races and castes in need of the rationality and efficiency that the West, particularly the Anglo-Saxon West, could provide. In essence, Kipling shared this view. At its highest it celebrated the good the English could do, often at great cost to themselves; at its worst, it supported and promoted a brutal racism.

The Indian characters in these short stories are usually marginal, and that very marginality speaks to an attitude about their insignificance in their own homeland. But Kipling does have stories in which the issue of race becomes paramount. In many, the narrator and the plot itself insist on an immutable barrier between the races and an assumption that the superiority of white blood over black or mixed blood is a fact of nature that cannot be eradicated. In fact, the few drops of white blood that temper the veins of the "borderline" people give them an authority over the totally black. In "His Chance in Life" (*PTH*), Kipling embodies this belief in Michele D'Cruze, a man of mixed blood, one who "looked down on natives as only a man with seven-eighths native blood in his veins can." Michele accepts, as all Indians in the story do, the superiority his drop of white blood affords him. When the town in which he works erupts in violence, Michele is the only inhabitant not totally black. The Native Police Inspector, recognizing Michele's status, calls him "Sahib" and awaits his order. His newly gained authority allows Michele to quell the disturbance. But when the young English Assistant Collector arrives, Michele loses his strength, bursts into tears of confusion, and relinquishes his authority. "It was the White drop in Michele's veins dying out, though he did not know it."

The racism in this story is not modified by any narrative commentary or tone. The reader is expected to understand that the different roles the English and Indians play are determined by differences of racial endowment. The English know how to assume command and direct others; the Indians break down in the face of difficulty. If one native does act nobly, it is his drop of white blood that allows it.

"Wee Willie Winkie" (*WWW*), another early story, also presents an unmodified racism. The eponymous young child rides out beyond the river that separates the territory of the Raj from Afghanistan to protect the impetuous young fiancée of his friend. Winkie emerges a hero when, after sending his horse back to the English cantonment as a signal for help, he stares down the Pathans menacing him and the injured girl. The story is sentimental in its affection for the child, but brutally stereotypical in its treatment of the English and the Afghan natives.

The helpless young English woman is surrounded by threatening black men; they refrain from capturing her when the English boy commands them, " 'I am the Colonel Sahib's son, and my order is that you go at once. You black men are frightening the Miss Sahib.' " For the natives know Winkie, part of the English world, implicitly commands the English troops; any harm done to him would be swiftly avenged. The six-year-old child displays the superior courage, and the Pathans retreat. They are made to seem rapacious in their instincts toward the young woman and boy, but cowardly when confronted with true English authority.

The story also presents a frequent image in Kipling's treatment of India, that of the boundary that separates the known and safe from the foreign and threatening. Here the river between India and Afghanistan serves as more than a physical demarcation; it separates what is permitted from what is forbidden. The contrast presents itself to Winkie in the fairy-tale language of his nursery book, George Macdonald's *The Princess and the Goblin*, "the bare black and purple hills across the river were inhabited by Goblins, and, in truth, every one had said that there lived the Bad Men." This childlike identification of the unknown natives with forces of evil is in no way undermined by the adults, however. Even Winkie's friend, the subaltern Brandis, has never traveled across the river. And the windows of Winkie's house are covered in paper to prevent the Bad Men from seeing in and taking aim. No wonder that, to Winkie, the river is "the end of all the

Earth." It marks the frontier where civilization and safety cease. But the language of magic and hyperbole called upon to describe this geographical territory turns it into a mythic land; the English become rescuing heroes and the natives subhuman villains.

Kipling has a handful of stories that present the differences between the English and the Indians in such stark and permanent terms. Yet when one surveys the many Anglo-Indian stories that focus on an Indian character, it becomes more difficult to define just one pervading point of view. Often a tale involves the affection between a British man and an Indian woman. The outcome is almost always disastrous, but the narrator's sympathies, from tale to tale, and even sometimes within a tale, are not always consistent or predictable.

An early story, "Kidnapped" (*PTH*), tells of a young subaltern, Peythroppe, honorable and esteemed, who inexplicably falls in love and proposes marriage to Miss Castries. The young lady, while possessing the highest qualities of character, is, everyone knows, unsuitable: she "possessed what innocent people at Home call a 'Spanish' complexion." "It was obviously absurd that Peythroppe should marry her. The little opal-tinted onyx at the base of her finger-nails said this as plainly as print." Miss Castries's complexion, revealed in her face and nails, speaks of her mixed blood. Peythroppe's friends conspire to have him granted, first a leave, then an extension, until finally the wedding day has passed and the humiliated Miss Castries has relinquished her ties to Peythroppe. The narrator looks forward, at the tale's conclusion, to Peythroppe's marrying "a sweet pink-and-white maiden" with money and position, "as every wise man should."

The story's tone, however, sits uneasily with the events it portrays. The narrator, a representative of the Anglo-Indian community, approves of all that transpires; he presents no alternative point of view. Yet he relates the events from a curious distance, almost tongue in cheek, an unspoken suggestion that the "everybody" who judges Miss Castries unfit, the "every wise man" who chooses only a socially approved mate, is facile and foolish. The "wise man" may be wise in the ways of the world, but seems morally shallow. The narrator's reiterated emphasis on the need for social propriety becomes more hollow as the story progresses. Overstatement intensifies the shakiness of public opinion. The narrator goes so far as to aver, "marriage in India does not concern the individual but the Government he serves." The more the narrator defends Peythroppe's friends, the more indefensible their actions seem. Kipling's story simultaneously defines and explodes the racism of these characters, all without a specific, overt criticism.

Many of the early Indian stories that treat the relationship between the races have a complex, iridescent hue. Some, like "Kidnapped," suggest a narrative irony; in others, the character most developed is Indian and the situation draws our sympathy. In "Lispeth" (*PTH*), the eponymous protagonist is a young Indian, a Hill girl, raised as a Christian and living as a servant-companion to the Chaplain's wife in a mission. Out walking one day, she comes upon a wounded young Englishman, brings him home, and nurses him back to health, intending to marry him when he recovers. The Englishman, amused by Lispeth's company, takes walks with her and showers her with attention. The dalliance means nothing to him; he is engaged to a girl back home. When he leaves, Lispeth waits patiently for months, confident he will return, until the Chaplain's wife admits the Englishman had no such intention.

The reader's sympathy is entirely with the Indian girl; orphaned in youth, rejected by her own people, patronized by a supercilious woman, deceived by a young Englishman, she has neither home nor friends. The narrator, less obvious a presence than in "Kidnapped," ironically speaks the language of those who have used Lispeth. She is "a savage by birth" and thus does not hide her feelings; she has "uncivilized Eastern instincts" and falls in love without forethought. But, again, such a characterization of Lispeth points out more the moral inadequacies of her judges than her own. While the other characters seem thoughtless and cruel, Lispeth is forthright and faithful. The young Indian girl emerges as far superior to the Anglo-Indians who surround her.

So, too, in "Georgie Porgie" (*LH*), the young Burmese girl whom Georgie, the Englishman, marries in a native ceremony proves faithful long after she has been abandoned. Georgie is happy with his native wife but thoughtlessly leaves her when he decides it is time to marry respectably. He brings his English bride to India, and the story closes with his Burmese wife finally discovering Georgie's treachery. The last sound we hear is that of her crying mingling with the dripping of a watercourse. No narrative comment urges us toward an interpretation, but Georgie is callous, his English wife shallow; only the Burmese girl acts out of love and fidelity.

And two of Kipling's most brilliant and memorable stories about the relationship between the races, again each treating an Englishman and a native woman, "Beyond the Pale" (*PTH*) and "Without Benefit of Clergy" (*LH*), approach the encounter with a troublingly clear-eyed understanding of the near impossibility of establishing permanent harmony between people in a culture whose existence depends on their separation. "Beyond the Pale" demonstrates the extraordinary talent Kipling showed from his earliest work. This brief tale is a masterpiece of control, rich in metaphor, spare and understated in diction. From its title, suggesting a stepping outside the appropriate political domain, to the social lie of its closing line, it investigates the dangers to body and spirit of moving beyond the sphere to which one is assigned. The opening sentences announce the need for confinement; "a man should, whatever happens, keep to his own caste, race, and breed. Let the White go to the White and the Black to the Black." The story depicts one who strays outside his boundary, and the narrator associates physical movement with intellectual transgression. "He knew too much."

Trejago, an English office worker, wanders into a blind alley one day and hears, behind a window grate, a pretty Indian voice speaking the words of a love poem. He finishes the verse for her, and thus begins their secret affair. She, a fifteen-year-old widow who lives with her uncle, has no contact with the outside world, and Trejago establishes a double life, spending his days at work in the Anglo-Indian community and his nights, after crawling through Bisesa's window, in her arms. Bisesa lives at the end of an alley, Amir Nath's Gully; the narrator's term for this cul de sac is "a trap." And she is kept behind a grated window, as if a prisoner, though hers is the only room in the gully with a window. She has enough access to the outside world to lure another or be caught by him. Trejago's progress is to move more deeply into the trap, from the gully, to her window, and into her room.

And Bisesa draws him in. After they speak for the first time, she sends him an object-letter, a cryptic message made of seeds, flowers, and bits of glass. Trejago knows how to interpret her invitation, and the narrator, whose opening lines were ominous, sounds his warning note: "no Englishman should be able to translate object-letters."

For Trejago, from the first, thinks he understands Bisesa's language. He knows her poem; he knows the code of her communication. He feels himself superior in this relationship, the one free to come and go, the one who controls whether or not they will meet, the one who seemingly knows her culture in a way she cannot know his. And her ignorance is insisted upon. She has difficulty pronouncing his

English name, but worse, cannot read the social codes of his world. Bisesa becomes wildly jealous because Trejago has been seen flirting with an English woman. Despite Trejago's attempts to reassure her, Bisesa will not be mollified. She recognizes only two states, fidelity and infidelity. The meaningless dalliances of social life, so much a part of Trejago's world, are foreign to hers. Nor can he really understand her distress.

In some way, mysterious to us, her anger seems to precipitate the story's violent conclusion. Trejago seeks her out again, but their love has been discovered. He finds Bisesa reaching out to him in the dark, with arms whose hands have been cut off at the wrists. Suddenly, from inside Bisesa's room, someone thrusts a knife; Trejago is wounded in the groin. Sometime later, after he recovers, he tries to find Bisesa again; he discovers the gully has been walled up and he does not know what Bisesa's house looks like from the other side. She is lost to him forever.

The trap has closed in on her. Kipling intensifies the image; her house is "as unknowable as the grave." But Bisesa's life has always been unknowable to Trejago. Thinking his experience of Indian life and the ways of the Anglo-Indian world gave him power, Trejago tries to erase the boundaries between the two domains. But Bisesa's passionate response to her misreading of Trejago's social rituals suggests the gulf that separates their mentalities, a void too great to be bridged. And her mutilating punishment, so horrifying to the reader, epitomizes the distance between her culture's values and ours. Trejago thought he understood her world, but, in important matters, he was as ignorant of hers as she was of his. His facility with the more accessible aspects of her culture, its poetry and traditions of object-letters, blinded him to a more profound ignorance of the values that sustain it. Her extramarital sexuality, her love for an Englishman, demand the highest punishment. She has stepped outside the morality prescribed for her and has paid with her hands, but Trejago moves back to his own world, where his slight limp is attributed to a mere riding accident. The difference between their fates marks the incommensurability of their cultures. Western society winks at events that are catastrophic in the East. As much as Trejago seemed to enter Bisesa's trap, he cannot. His culture protects him. The walled-up Amir Nath's Gully stands as an image of the impenetrability of Indian culture to the Western mind.

The cultural division between the races is Kipling's vehicle for exploring a concern that, while secondary to him, has come to dominate much modern literature, the subjective nature of reality: the belief that we are prisoners of our own perceptions, our own idiosyncratic ways of interpreting those perceptions; we cannot escape into another's mind and share his or her view of the world; we cannot know anything for certain. Kipling does not press his treatment of racial differences to that conclusion, but his stories often do suggest the unknowability of others' experience, first in his use of unreliable or ironic narrators, and second in his treatment of the insurmountable barriers to a full intellectual and spiritual communion between the East and the West.

"Without Benefit of Clergy," like "Beyond the Pale," works with barriers and boundaries and enclosed spaces, but to very different effect. Again we pass from the vague, relatively undefined outside world of the Anglo-Indian civil servant into the private world of the Indian, but Kipling's descriptions are much more specific here. We move into the red-walled city, through the courtyard, past a wooden gate to the house of Ameera, the sixteen-year-old girl John Holden bought two years before the story begins. But Ameera's room is no prison, and she is no mere courtesan; the narrator insists the room is a palace and that Holden and Ameera are king and queen.

These two create their own world, and it is richly described. We see the bedroom's furnishings, its red-lacquered couch, floor cloths, and cushions. We are given an elaborate portrait of Ameera wearing her best clothes, her diamond nose stud, the flawed emeralds and rubies in her forehead ornament, her gold necklace and silver anklets, her jade-green muslin gown. Though she is poor, we see Ameera through her own and Holden's eyes, shining in color and grace, and deeply happy. And at night, she and Holden and their infant son, Tota, climb to the roof of the house to count the stars. The celestial system itself becomes part of the kingdom Ameera and Holden create.

But Holden leads a double life. He spends his nights with Ameera in the house he rents for her and his days at work. Yet his public existence has little meaning for Holden; he enjoys the club life, to be sure, but his work is unsatisfying, a distraction, something he performs poorly and cares little for. He rushes home at the end of each day to Ameera, and the grayness of his public days is contrasted with the intense color of his private nights.

But Holden and Ameera's life together is doomed. Although she fears Holden must eventually return to the English world, take an English wife, and leave his Indian idyll behind, Ameera does not live to see her fears realized. First Tota becomes ill and dies of "the seasonal autumn fever." Kipling's term, so matter of fact, makes Tota's death seem one of many, almost to be expected. Though Ameera and Holden do their best to comfort each other, the rigors of the Indian climate attack again. Cholera becomes epidemic. Because their life is secret and unsanctioned by the government, Holden cannot send Ameera to the hill station for protection. His efforts to persuade her to go on her own to the mountains are unsuccessful. She prides herself on a fidelity that surpasses that of the self-absorbed English women. She stays in the city, contracts the disease, and dies in Holden's arms.

From the beginning of the story, Ameera and Holden have tried to appeal to and placate the gods. She especially prays for a son, prays for a healthy child, prays that her life be taken before Holden's or the child's. But the gods do not protect Ameera; nor does nature, which brings drought and disease; nor does society, which despises such as her. The forces that surround the life she creates with Holden pierce the boundaries, enter the house, and destroy what is valuable within. In her dying words, Ameera forswears those things in which she formerly placed her trust, amulets and charms, rituals and prayer. " 'I bear witness—I bear witness'—the lips were forming the words on his ear—'that there is no God but—thee, beloved!' " Only the personal life they have created is of value to Ameera. No force outside their love can protect or comfort.

As Ameera dies, the long-awaited rains arrive with torrents of water and driving winds. Three days later, Holden, who is about to be transferred, returns to Ameera's house. It has been beaten down by the deluge, the pillars destroyed, the gate torn from its hinge, "as if the house had been untenanted for thirty years instead of three days." For it was Ameera who animated the house; she, like Holden, possessed the spark of divinity that gives life. Without her, the house collapses. Holden's landlord declares, in sympathy, that he will tear down any part that remains standing, "so that no man may say where this house stood." All evidence of the love Ameera and Holden bore each other will be obliterated.

The story uncompromisingly elevates the dignity and value of the private love Ameera and Holden share over any external set of conventions. Here is a world where, seemingly, the social structures that

separate the races are surmountable. But the victory, though profound, is evanescent. For the Indian girl and Anglo-Indian man live in
a world where outside forces ultimately reign. Kipling's story does not
patronize or infantilize the Indian; rather, Ameera teaches Holden the
sanctity of the inner life, the hollowness of the outer. But both characters are fated to suffer. For the private world cannot long endure without the support of the public. The secrecy of Holden's family life
means he is continually separated from Ameera; he is, in his superi-
or's eyes, a bachelor, easily transferred to new posts when a short-term
substitute is needed. And the structures that would have helped Ameera
and Tota, removal to a better climate, medical care, are unavailable to
this clandestine family. If Ameera and Holden's love seems sweeter
because it is private, its narrow circumscription makes it vulnerable
and intensifies its pain. At the story's end, in his suffering, Holden
must yet go back to work alone, unable to speak of the disaster his life
has become.

Kipling's images of space and enclosure define a protected place
where private safety and pleasure can exist apart from a threatening
frontier. Most often, in the Indian stories, the enclosed space is that of
the Raj. But here he reverses the pattern; it is the public world that
threatens this private garden where psychic identity and joy can exist.
The legally sanctioned world is barren; the illegitimate is sacred. And
Kipling's title becomes ironic; Ameera and Holden reject the favors of
convention. They suffer the mortal consequences, but their happiness
surpasses any other even hinted at in the public world.

A story such as "Without Benefit of Clergy" undermines any attempt to interpret Kipling's view of the Empire as mere racist exploitation. There is no doubt he has many racist stories, that he often
portrays Indians as children, incapable of making mature judgments
about their lives, as intellectually inferior, morally primitive, emotion-
ally unstable. There is no doubt, too, that his major sympathies were
with the English who traveled to India, often for mixed motives, but
who were capable of great sacrifice and great good. But he also wrote
of the hidden lives of Indians, of deep and lasting affection among
lovers and families, of the hardships endured by those who live the
lives of a subjugated people. Moreover, these stories, among those
with Indian settings, contain virtually Kipling's only treatment of a
rich and satisfying sexuality. The sexual drive of Kipling's Anglo-
Indian characters seems feeble, narrow, and manipulative compared
with that of his Indians. There is no Anglo-Indian equivalent to Ameera,

whose inner sensuousness, complemented by her physical beauty, is fully integrated with her affections and becomes the mainstay of her life.

Some of Kipling's stories are hard to read today. They celebrate a point of view we find forbidding. But he is an artist with a rich sympathy for India and for those westerners who went out there to work. Ultimately, his view of the Empire, based on respect for practical labor, recognition of the value of community, belief in political order and social stability, is positive. But his profound understanding, evidenced in many stories, of the pain inflicted by imperialism, humanizes his beliefs. The existence of stories that treat that pain with tenderness must stand as a testimony to the complexity of Kipling's writings about the Empire.

Myth and History

During the middle years of his career, while still writing of India and of war, and increasingly of England, Kipling produced a group of short stories, later collected as the *Jungle Book*, the *Second Jungle Book, Just So Stories, Puck of Pook's Hill,* and *Rewards and Fairies,* that have come to be considered children's books. Some of these stories were, in fact, written for Kipling's own children; indeed, in some, main characters are thinly veiled versions of those children. Although in subject matter and style, many often recognize children's tastes, they are not for the most part childlike in either thematic concern or manner. With the exception of the *Just So Stories,* the simplest of the group, they regularly consider the interests and expectations of a mature audience. In his autobiography, *Something of Myself,* Kipling says of *Rewards and Fairies,* "the tales had to be read by children, before people realised that they were meant for grown-ups" (111). The same may be said of most of the other children's stories.

One reason for the power of these stories is that they reveal Kipling's propensity for what Bonamy Dobrée calls a "fabulist" mode of literature.[13] They move toward the realm of myth, and they do so in Kipling's habitual manner, conjoining a minutely detailed creation of natural fact with an urge for the fantastic. The result is that these stories, particularly the Jungle Books and the Puck tales, *Puck of Pook's Hill* and *Rewards and Fairies,* create a world fully believable in its lineaments and color, and yet a world where animals talk and the long-dead walk the earth again.

Throughout his middle years, Kipling wrote many stories we might term anthropomorphic. He has a group, for example, in which inanimate objects talk to each other. In "The Ship that Found Herself," the individual parts of the vessel learn to work together, conversing as they go, in order to fashion a successful operating machine. In "—007," locomotives urge on and support each other. And he has numerous stories in which animals speak. In "Below the Mill Dam" (*T&D*), a rat and cat as well as a wheel and the water bicker over the impending arrival of electricity, an event that presages doom to their way of life, though they do not know it. This last story is often considered a political allegory, a confrontation between the older, leisured, conservative classes and the busy, utilitarian, newer forces.[14] So too "The Mother Hive" (*A&R*) uses the habits of bees to make political points about useful toil.

These relatively minor stories indicate Kipling's interest in giving a voice to the inanimate or inarticulate, making them represent some human points of view, but they do not show the imaginative depth he could find in this strain, nor the far-reaching moral vision that underlies his best efforts. The children's collections, though different from each other in setting, in characters, and in ostensible thematic concern, reveal not only an instinct to humanize nature, both landscape and animal life, but an importing of moral meaning into objects and events usually considered amoral, as well as a persistent interest in origins and history.

The *Just So Stories for Little Children*, the collection's full title, remains perhaps the work of Kipling's most fully accommodated to a child's mind and the one still read primarily by or to children. These short tales are, in their own way, about the origin of species, but Kipling calls on a child's curiosity and fear and sense of justice to explain the perplexing world that surrounds his young audience. J. I. M. Stewart has called them "little myths solving little riddles"[15]; the stories explain the causes of strange facts in the natural and finally intellectual world.

"How the Whale Got His Throat" introduces the collection and sets its tone, humorous and affectionate; but we are also alerted to the fact that we are entering a dangerous universe where whales devour the unsuspecting. It is only after being swallowed by the Whale and subsequently jumping and dancing to cause the animal to hiccough that the wily mariner escapes. He leaves behind his suspenders, and the narrator's refrain to his listener, "you must *not* forget the suspenders, Best Beloved," becomes comprehensible. For the mariner breaks up the raft on which he had floated into the whale's mouth, and, using his suspenders, ties its slats together in a vertical and horizontal pattern, creating a grate; finally, he lodges the grate in the whale's throat, preventing the predatory animal from ever again devouring so large an object as a man. The clever human being outwits the animal, a pattern repeated in many of these stories.

"How the Rhinoceros Got His Skin" pits the somewhat mysterious Parsee against the frightening Rhinoceros. The Parsee, living alone by the Red Sea, discovers that his cake, his magnificent baked creation, has been stolen and consumed by the rude, greedy animal. But the Parsee has his revenge; when, one hot day, the Rhinoceros sheds his smoothly fitting skin in order to bathe, the Parsee fills the skin with cake crumbs. The itchy, uncomfortable Rhinoceros, trying to get rid of the crumbs, stretches and pulls his skin until it resembles the baggy suit it is today. This tale, like the others in the collection, gives a sensible, though ludicrous, explanation of an unusual observable fact. Although the narrator draws on a child's sense of fair play in choosing the Parsee's side, both characters retain a dangerous power. The Parsee, with his extraordinary hat, from which "the rays of the sun were reflected in more-than-oriental splendour," and his cooking stove, "of the kind that you must particularly never touch," suggest the magician or perhaps the artist; allied with light and color and warmth, working at the edge of safety, he creates a cake whose glory far surpasses its meager nutritional, utilitarian value. Indeed, he bakes not the staff of life but dessert, unnecessary but desirable for its delicate sensuousness. And the great force of nature, the Rhinoceros, devours it. But although the Parsee triumphs, the reader feels both characters retain their ability to threaten the other. In general, these stories, while domesticating animals sufficiently to make their lives understandable, do not entirely tame them. And their enduring strangeness accounts for part of the collection's charm.

Kipling's interest in the origins of the animals' appearance and behavior culminates in "The Crab that Played with the Sea," which takes place at the beginning of time when the "Eldest Magician was getting Things ready." He prepares the earth and the sea and brings the animals out to play. As each primary animal spontaneously finds his appropriate activity, the geography of the world springs up. The mounds of earth tossed out by the Elephant as he digs with his tusks become the Himalayan mountains; the rocks the Turtle whirls through the air into the sea become the islands of the Malay Archipelago. And the sullen, uncooperative Crab, who digs a hole in the sea, leaving it twice a day to search for food, causes the tides as his burrow first draws and then repels water. Even man finds himself affected by all these activities, especially the movement of the tides. This tale, like others in the collection, balances a gently humorous tone with a respect for the power and potential danger of the animals. The natural world here is somewhat unpredictable and always a little threatening; it has been created, we are reminded, by a great magician.

There is a distinct human presence in this tale, however, a man, Son of Adam he is called, and his companion, here not a mate but "his own best-beloved little girl-daughter." The father-daughter relationship is intense in these stories, particularly affecting when one knows Kipling's favorite child, his first daughter, Josephine, died at the age of six in 1899, three years before these tales were published. Her presence breathes through them, many of which were composed for and read aloud to her and her brother. The little girl and her father in this story are endangered by the tides, but, aided by the Magician and their own wit and courage, they subdue the Crab sufficiently so that, although he can still act, he can do so only within certain limits. Human beings, like the Man and his daughter and the Parsee, form an unstable truce with the natural world. In these tales, the human wins, but failure is always near and possible. The joyful tone is not mindless.

But it can be sentimental. In "How the Alphabet Was Made," a father and daughter, devoted to each other, together create the first alphabet, a series of pictures, designs based on natural shapes, to correspond with vowel and consonant sounds. The ingenuity of the alphabet's forms is set against affectionate family scenes. The father's excitement at what he has discovered is balanced by the child's boredom at these pedantic exercises. But together they create what the father terms "*the* big secret of the world," how to communicate to one who is absent. But this is a book of secrets, the ancient hidden origins of the world as we know it, all revealed to the reader in an engaging tone.

It is a world where animals can think and talk, where human beings live close to the magical, creative power of life, where beauty and danger are intertwined, in short, a child's world. Throughout, Kipling maintains a tone of wonder and discovery. These stories remain enchanting fables, often with an implicit or explicit moral. They touch on adult concerns, survival and revenge and the development of writing, but do not seriously probe any of them.

The Jungle Books approach their subjects quite differently. Still Kipling's most popular work, these stories have traditionally been thought of by readers as the Mowgli and non-Mowgli tales.[16] The Mowgli stories tell of the young boy, abandoned by his parents and raised by wolves. Nurtured and taught by the jungle animals, he eventually becomes Master of the Jungle. But, as he enters young manhood, he finds his human instincts pulling him back to the world of civilization, a world he has entered into only a few times in his life, and always with unhappy results. The *Second Jungle Book* closes as Mowgli prepares, ambivalently, to return to the human world. In a story not published as part of the Jungle Books, "In the Rukh" (*MI*), we catch a last glimpse of Mowgli, in society, married, working as a forest ranger. But this story, though treating the later phase of Mowgli's life, was actually written before the Jungle Book tales. And it is a feeble anticipation of the imaginative power of the Jungle Books themselves; its Mowgli is almost a parody of civilized man.[17] It is rather in the great Jungle Book stories that we see the richness of Kipling's portraits of jungle life and the complexity of his view of the relationship between human beings and the natural world they inhabit. Unlike the *Just So Stories*, the Mowgli tales at times might seem to blur the distinctions between human and animal nature. Mowgli is raised in the animal world, taught by animal protectors; he speaks their language, including the different dialects of the different species. But Mowgli is recognized from the first as "a man's cub" ("Mowgli's Brothers," *JB*), distinct in both actuality and potential from those around him. His distinction endows Mowgli's story with pathos; though he does not know it, the animals surrounding Mowgli intuit that one day he must leave the jungle; "Man goes to Man at the last" ("Letting in the Jungle," *SJB*). Despite the fact that he is the "little brother" to the animals, he possesses powers they do not. Their eyes cannot meet his; his glance is authoritative. He comes to learn not only the language of animals, but human language, something his brothers in the jungle can never do. And he is unafraid of fire, the great threat to the jungle. These marks of his difference portend his different fate.

But it would be a diminution of their imaginative power to see the Mowgli stories merely as a study of the distinctions between the human and the wild. They are a bildungsroman, a study almost archetypal of growing up; of being tutored, as Wordsworth was, by beauty and by fear; of primal joy that must be left in order to enter the civilized world. And they are profoundly engaging stories, with a compelling narrative drive, with developed, sympathetic characters, and with vivid natural settings.

Because the Mowgli tales focus on a group of characters who reappear in story after story, and because they trace the maturing of a central figure over the course of many stories, it may be helpful to examine them not only as individual tales but as a treatment of a handful of consistent, overarching themes. One way of sorting out some of the different strands that make up the stories is to concentrate on the Law of the Jungle, Kipling's conception of a particular structure that gives coherence to the community.

Such coherence is an abiding concern of Kipling's, apparent in much of his work, and here, of course, the issue is framed in a special blend of natural history and myth, a story of a child and his animal friends, told with affection and yet an eye to zoological and geographical detail. Nevertheless, the Law crosses the border between the human and the nonhuman and can help us see both the connections and demarcations between them. Moreover, internalizing the Law is one of the ways Mowgli comes to understand himself and his responsibility for the consequences of his actions, and our witnessing his education in the Law can help us trace his development. The Law is a pervasive, inclusive code of behavior that governs the lives of these animals who live along the banks of the Waingunga River in Central India. Mowgli must learn the Law from Baloo, the old bear who teaches it to the wolf cubs as well. But the Law is largely instinctive to the animals; Mowgli must be taught meticulously and repeatedly. Whereas the animals need know only those aspects of the Law that pertain to their welfare, Mowgli must learn enough of the Law and the language of all species to protect him from the dangerous consequences of being an outsider with no instinctive guide.

In "Mowgli's Brothers," we are introduced to the human child, just able to walk, who is adopted by Mother and Father Wolf. Presumably left behind by his parents in a moment of panic when they were surrounded by menacing animals, Mowgli himself is pursued by Shere Khan, the ruthless tiger. He is taken into the wolves' lair to be protected as one of their own. And, in an elaborate communal ceremony, he is presented to the entire pack to be recognized and protected; he becomes the "little brother" to the wolves and their friends. The story leaps forward ten or eleven years, and we see Mowgli in his strong preadolescent youth, a period that is the focus of the Jungle Books; he is being instructed, as he has been for years, in jungle practices by Baloo and the black panther, Bagheera. And in the course of the story, particularly in the Pack Council and Baloo's lessons, we are introduced to the jungle world, its material life and its codes.

The jungle is ruled by the Law, and Baloo advises Mowgli in "How Fear Came" (*SJB*) that "the Law was like the Giant Creeper, because it dropped across every one's back and no one could escape." The Law is universal in the jungle; the animals know it and must abide by it. Only Mowgli has no instinctive knowledge; he must be entirely taught. Yet Kipling, by making Baloo the teacher of the young wolves as well, makes the Law something that is not purely instinctive; it is communicated by teaching and example.

The Law, we are told in "Mowgli's Brothers," "never orders anything without a reason." And there is, as one might expect, one reason that underlies all others, survival. But, as many commentators have pointed out, Kipling's concept of the Law of the Jungle is almost the exact opposite of what the term is usually thought to mean; it is not aggressive personal survival or anarchic wilfulness (see, for example Stewart, 142–43). As this story and others in the series make clear, the jungle is a community, at times an overly idealized community to be sure, but one in which the preservation of the pack or the species is a persistent motive. The pack acts to protect its own, all of its own; Mowgli as an adopted member must be physically recognized so that he will not be attacked. Indeed, all the young cubs are inspected and identified so that they can run free until they are old enough to defend themselves. The pack profits from looking after its young.

The wolf pack is repeatedly termed the Free People; the wolves define themselves and are known by others in this way. And their freedom is marked by obedience to the leader, the Head of the Pack, who maintains his authority by strength and cunning. His power gives direction and cohesion to the pack; the wolves are proud of their strength and respected by the other animals. By their actions they help to maintain order and hierarchy in the jungle. But when their leader, Akela, grows old and can no longer kill, an act necessary to prove his power and protectiveness, the wolves reject him. They strike out on their own, following their individual desires. The result is that the pack loses its reason for being. Finally, injured from traps and ill from bad food, the wolves seek out their old leader and his defender, Mowgli. In " 'Tiger-Tiger!' " (*JB*), they cry out, "Lead us again, O Akela. Lead us again, O Man-cub, for we be sick of this lawlessness, and we would be the Free People once more."

The wolves' lives demonstrate Kipling's view of the connection between obedience to authority, physical well-being, and social cohesion. The Law of the Jungle defines the places of animals within the pack; the strength that derives from this communal organization gives them power and freedom. They defer to no one but their own leader, who merits respect by his proven ability. Akela rules beyond his earned time because he is supported by Mowgli, who loves him. But the Law demands that Akela relinquish his power when he can no longer wield it for the common good. And in "Red Dog" (*SJB*), after a fierce and noble last battle, the aged wolf sings his Death Song.

The importance of authority and cohesion is examined from another perspective in "How Fear Came." The tale begins by describing a drought in the jungle, one which necessitates the animals' invoking the Water Truce, a period of peace when the hunting that constitutes daily life ceases and all animals are secure. They may, without fear of attack, approach the only source of water remaining, drink their fill of the now foul water, and proceed quietly back to their homes. No one may kill another when the Truce is called; in their mutual suffering, the animals refrain from killing each other, for, by so doing, each is insured a drink in peace. And the Law deems that anyone who breaks the Truce must suffer death.

But Kipling's description of the Water Truce provides a background for and commentary on the main concern of the story: the animals' myth of a prelapsarian jungle. The story is told by Hathi, the wild elephant, of the beginning of the jungle, when animals lived together without fear because no animal was hunted or endangered; they ate only fruits and flowers, grass and bark. But, in a gesture of anger and impatience, the tiger accidently killed a buck, bringing Death into the jungle. As a punishment, the tiger lost his position as master and judge and was replaced by the Gray Ape. But this successor proved incompetent, and the jungle, leaderless, was left confused. It was then that Tha, the first of the elephants and the Lord of the Jungle, created a new order. He introduced Fear, in the person of Man. "Now it is time there was a Law, and a Law that ye must not break. Now ye shall know Fear, and when ye have found him ye shall know that he is your master." The animals encountered Man, the hairless one who walks on his hind legs, and ran away in terror. From that time on, the animals have lived in a tense uneasiness, for Man, with intellect, imagination, tools, and especially fire, can, though physically weaker, outthink and outmaneuver the jungle people. Moreover, Man is unpredictable; as Mowgli laments in "Letting in the Jungle" (*SJB*), men are cruel; they kill for sport, not simply for food; they torture their own kind. To the animals, Man is powerful and threatening, and his physical inferiority is a snare; once attacked, he can wreak havoc in revenge.

The jungle here is very different from the world of the *Just So Stories*. To jungle animals, issues of fear, imminent death, power, and authority are constant. There can be no relaxing of one's guard. The *Just*

So Stories may imply a dangerous world, but we do not see it. In the Jungle Books we see slaughter and the eating of one's prey; we see animals stripped and their hides displayed in triumph. We have moved into a world where the mortal threats that compose so much of life are vividly present.

We see that the Law is undergirded by fear. The animals abide by the codes of the jungle to protect themselves and their kind against each other and most particularly against Man. Their society becomes a fragile structure built by the animals against an irrational enemy, one who acts mercilessly and without regard to consequence. The structure is hierarchical and protective. Authority rests on merit, compels obedience, and offers security.

"How Fear Came" is a complex tale, a story within a story. We are introduced to the thirst of the animals, the paucity of fruits and berries resulting in hunger, the misery that follows from drought in a hot climate. The timid enervation of the animals as they approach the river, looking carefully to make sure no one violates the Water Truce, adds to the unnaturalness of the situation. The jungle is exhausted, and the dead lie everywhere. Indeed, this night Shere Khan, the tiger, has asserted his right, granted once a year, to approach Man fearlessly. He has killed a man, and the jungle tensely awaits the retribution. Within this physical and emotional anxiety, Hathi the elephant tells his story of the world's beginning—idyllic, peaceful, without danger or fear. The Edenic earth of which Hathi speaks stands in painful contrast to the actual world Mowgli and his animal friends now inhabit. But the tale is more than just contrasting scenes; it demonstrates how both the suffering and the release, the pain of drought and the Truce that allows the animals to drink, derive from the introduction of Death into the jungle. The earth changed when Death came, but Death brought the need for Law, and it is this common code that gives the animals a way to deal with their suffering.

Kipling's story, which at first seems to contain a frame for an inner tale, turns out to have numerous interweavings between the outer and inner narrative. Not so much a frame as a border, constructed of the same material and using the same colors and motifs of the tale it surrounds, the outer tale, to which we return at the end, is necessary for an understanding of the implications of the inner; the prelapsarian world can only be understood when the consequences of its acts are vividly presented.

The Law of the Jungle, in its universal application, its protective ability, seems the animals' best response to a threatening world. And Kipling makes clear the consequences of living without the Law. In "Kaa's Hunting" (*JB*), he gives an elaborate example of the breakdown of authority and community. The story begins with Baloo's teaching Mowgli the Master Words of the Jungle, those by which he can claim protection from all the animals. "We be of one blood, ye and I," Mowgli repeats, asserting his oneness with all the beasts, and Baloo teaches him to say the words in all the different languages heard in the jungle.

But Mowgli has encountered one group of whom Baloo heartily disapproves, the Bander-log, the Monkey-People. Bagheera, too, is angry; "the people without a Law," he terms them. For the Bander-log possess a number of characteristics the other animals deem hateful. They live in trees, and because they can flit from one to the next in easy escape, they have no healthy sense of fear. Thus they tease and torment others without regard to consequences. They have no native tongue, no dignity of utterance; their language is a hodge-podge of words they have heard others speak. They have no leader; they act on someone's whim, change their minds, and accede to another's whim. And they have no memory, no goals, no fidelity to plans. These useless, rootless, friendless, chattering animals embody the antithesis of those qualities the jungle admires and promotes. And in the course of the tale, the Bander-log kidnap Mowgli and we see at close range what it means to be lawless in the jungle.

Without a leader, the Bander-log are not a Free People like the wolves; they are a mob. They snatch Mowgli as he naps and take him to the Cold Lairs, the mysterious ruins of an ancient human city now overgrown. Kipling's description of the Bander-log in Cold Lairs is vivid and memorable. Amidst the roofless houses and marble fragments of a palace, the monkeys play at being human; they sit in circles and chatter, as if in council. Finally, like overtired children, they grow weary and begin to quarrel. Mowgli cannot understand them; their play is purposeless and destructive; they cannot organize themselves sufficiently to collect food. Mowgli fears he will be starved or killed. And, indeed, having stolen him, the Bander-log have no idea what to do with him. They imprison Mowgli, who begins to despair of escape.

He is saved, however, by Baloo, Bagheera, and their powerful ally, Kaa, the python. The monkeys are beaten and disperse, and Mowgli returns to his friends. But he is punished for his heedlessness and his minimizing of the great sacrifice the other animals made on his behalf. For punishment too is part of the Law.

The Bander-log present a powerful contradiction to the Law's values. And, indeed, it has been argued the monkeys are Kipling's satiric attack on human tendencies toward irresponsibility, insolence, fecklessness; they represent the chattering, ineffectual aspects of us all, that which cannot or will not act in an ordered, moral manner, the lazy, fruitless strain that leads to chaos and mad laughter.[18] Kipling has other portraits of characters so disorganized as to be self-destructive, but the Bander-log, distanced from us by their animal nature, allow us to see these qualities in an antic mirror. They ultimately fail, and their lawlessness is their weakness, but they do present an ever-present threat to the jungle.

Kipling's Law of the Jungle is natural law. For the most part, the animals are born with an instinct for behavior that promotes survival. Kipling humanizes the creatures by indicating that their young must patiently learn the Law from their elders and that animals are punished if they break the rules. Indeed, some animals, notably Shere Khan, seem to take a Man-like pleasure in killing. But, for the most part, Kipling's animal world, while analogous to the human, is not identical to it. Mowgli's existence, at the threshold between the human and the animal, attests to the difference between the two. Although he loves the animals and is loved in turn, his rationality and imagination distinguish him from them and make him their master. But the animals also intuit in Mowgli's superiority a threat to their lives; the astute defer to him. Those who do not suffer mortal consequences.

It has been argued that Kipling imposes a consistency, indeed a morality, upon the animal world, that he treats instinctive behavior as if it were freely chosen (Stewart, 143–45). And to some extent the criticism is just. His conversing, affectionate animals, however, still retain an amoral and lethal dignity. The predatory nature of jungle behavior is never far from the scene in the Jungle Books. Toward the end of "Kaa's Hunting," the python performs his mesmerizing Dance of the Hunger of Kaa, a sinuous captivation of the monkeys that will result in their destruction. This is a world of wildlife.

But there is no doubt that the elements that work together to best secure survival, the strong community, the role of authority, the protection of the young, the necessity for rank and order, the rules for hunting and killing, all have a moral dimension that make these stories a fable of human life. The emphasis on the common good, moderation, respect for elders, care for the weak, perseverance in fulfilling tasks, all are human virtues that can be read as supported and developed by the Law. No transcendent system existing outside the animals' efforts, but an accreted, practical set of commands for sustaining communal and individual life, the Law is a version of Kipling's faith in the necessity of structure, harmony, and community in all life. By anchoring the Law in animal life, Kipling makes its conservative values natural, undeniable, and inevitable. To reject them makes one seem destructive and anarchic, akin to the Bander-log.

But Mowgli embodies another strain in human nature. The uniform code that is the Law cannot entirely include him; his intellectual superiority and imaginative independence prevent it; while part of the natural world, and largely bound by its codes, he is yet outside it as well. This fact is both his glory and his burden. And the poignancy of his departure, at the end of the Jungle Books, for the world of men and women, attests to the boy's distinctness. In the Jungle Books, the spark that separates the human from the animal is a mixed blessing, and the good uses to which that spark may be put are not explored. Mowgli's intelligence enables him to save his fellow animals, but that intelligence seems fierce and inflexible. Virtually all nourishing, affirming emotion in these stories rests in the animal world. So too do the stability and security that derive from living within the Law. Our few glimpses of human society introduce us to a restless, aggressive world where pride and revenge are powerful, where human beings treat each other cruelly to protect their vanity, a world from which Mowgli instinctively recoils and which he must, in time, learn to reenter. Mowgli's education in the Law of the Jungle seems a great gift he brings with him as he approaches the tangled and unpredictable morality of the human world.

In *Puck of Pook's Hill* and *Rewards and Fairies*, Kipling's fabulist tendencies take a different turn. Although nature is important and powerful in these stories, it is not dangerous; it is neither the sea nor the jungle, but the gentle Sussex weald, the coasts of southern England, the rolling hills of Pennsylvania. It is nature domesticated to human needs and uses, an assumed background rather than a problematic focus. And human nature is assumed as well. We do not explore its limits or take its measure against the animal world. The stories in these two volumes view men and women in their human community. The reader is not poised at the beginning of time when species emerge or at the beginning of human thought when a figure defines himself against the natural world. Instead, we step in and out of history, concerned not with origins or boundaries but with development and continuity.

And yet these books too exist in the realm of the fantastic. Kipling's conceit is the figure of Puck. Bearing his mythological and literary associations, the woodland sprite appears to two modern children living in Sussex. Teaching the boy and girl, Dan and Una, amusing them, piquing their interest, satisfying their curiosity, he conjures up a series of figures from the past, men and women who once walked the same ground as they. These historical characters, from the Viking raids, the Roman occupation, the Norman conquest, the Tudor dynasty, from a myriad of times and backgrounds, appear to the children, emerging on the landscape to tell their life stories. As the children hear the history of their country, of their own little plot of land, they are drawn into a deeper communion with the spirit that constitutes Englishness. Kipling, who in his lifetime lived in Europe and America, India and Africa, had, at the time of these stories, settled in the very landscape he is describing. The tales are, in part, a praise of the English countryside, more powerful perhaps because coming from the intense imagination of one who never felt fully at home anywhere.

In the first tale in *Puck of Pook's Hill*, "Weland's Sword," we are introduced to Dan and Una, who, on Midsummer Eve, are acting passages from *A Midsummer Night's Dream*. Sitting in a fairy ring near Pook's Hill, an ancient and well-known site, they look up to find Puck himself, the faunlike character of art and legend, approaching them. On this enchanted night, traditionally the time of fairies and spirits, the children's interlacing of landscape, myth, and literature has been so powerful that Puck exclaims, "You've broken the Hills! It hasn't happened in a thousand years." The children have inadvertently opened up the silence of the earth, broken through the mundane into the magical, called forth the past into the present, the spiritual into the physical. Puck has been conjured up and he, in turn, will in the stories of these two volumes evoke others, introducing the children to the hidden life that lies around them, teaching them they are part of the continuum of time, that the past is not dead but rather lives within the present.

One of the first things Puck does is cut a clod from the land and hand it to the children, "taking seizin,' " it is called, an old custom of giving a piece of land to a new buyer; you do not truly own the land until the seller gives you a handful of it, until you have seized it. In a sense, Dan and Una spend these two volumes truly seizing their land. That which was a token in a commercial transaction becomes deeply symbolic. The children take possession of the land's history, its facts and legends, as a preparation for inheriting its future. They learn how to become its faithful stewards, to realize its permanence and their own transitoriness.

The sword of the story's title was fashioned by Wayland-Smith, the blacksmith who is, in fact, the norse god Weland. The norsemen brought their gods with them to England, Puck explains. But the gods required harsh sacrifices, human as well as animal, and people grew weary of such demands. Becoming bolder, losing their fear of the gods, they began to mimic sacrifice rather than perform it. The gods themselves, dependent on human belief for their strength, began to dwindle into demigods and human beings. Though still possessed of unusual powers, these diminished beings lived a captive existence, unhappy but unable to alter their state. Finally, Weland is thanked for his work by a young man and thereby released from his drudgery and allowed to return to Valhalla. But first he repays his well-wisher by creating for him a magical sword, carved with runes and endowed with the power of singing out in warning, in rejoicing, in mourning, that is, in participating in the life of its master.

Weland's deliverer, Hugh, a young Saxon, uses the sword to defend himself against the invading Normans. But in the next three tales, "Young Men at the Manor," "The Knights of the Joyous Venture," and "Old Men at Pevensey," and in "The Tree of Justice" in *Rewards and Fairies*, we see the sword become an instrument not of destruction but of salvation and friendship. Although the Norman tales begin with the Battle of Hastings and the animosities between the conqueror and the conquered, the true story they narrate is one of building a country, of reconciliation and cooperation. As the great Norman knight De Aquila prophesizes, "in fifty years there will be neither Norman nor Saxon, but all English" ("Old Men at Pevensey").

The primary mode of building an English community out of warring factions is by securing and working the land. In "Young Men at the Manor," we see Sir Richard Dalyngridge, a Norman, take possession of the Manor usurped from Hugh, Weland's savior. But Sir Richard and Hugh join forces to protect the land from thieves and marauders of all political allegiances. They guard the valley, fell the timber, run the mill, feed the grazing sheep, fish the ponds, repair thatched cottages, keep the books, in short, learn by sheer toil the intricacies of the land they govern. And by performing these acts, they win the affection of all who live on the Manor. They overcome the divisions of politics by arduous labor for the common good. And Sir Richard, the interloper, learns to love the land; "I set out to conquer England three days after I was made knight. I did not then know that England would conquer me."

In "Old Men at Pevensey," we see Sir Richard and the now-knighted Sir Hugh in their old age. Having followed them through many adventures, we watch their last attempts to save their beloved Sussex lands from still another Norman attack. For they are now thoroughly at one in their Englishness and their belief in the rightness of a native king. These Norman tales, spoken to the children by Sir Richard as he appears to them walking his horse through the woods, celebrate the power of work and friendship and love of the land. They also touch on a secondary theme that runs through the Puck volumes; the invader can fall in love with the land he invades, become subject to its richness and its rhythms, and finally become as much a part of it as the native. The invader can contribute, as Sir Richard and De Aquila do, but his greatest contribution is also his greatest reward, to become at home in the land he inhabits, not dominating but sharing it with those who have always lived there.

In *Puck of Pook's Hill*, the children meet another member of an occupying army, the British-born Roman centurion Parnesius. In three stories, "A Centurion of the Thirtieth," "On the Great Wall," and "The Winged Hats," we trace Parnesius's career from a young boy entering military service to an old veteran of many years defending Hadrian's Wall. Parnesius has traveled across the children's land and knows their mill, but his true experience has been on the Wall. He describes it in detail, its thickness, its views, the town that has grown up behind it. But he has been sent to the Wall as a result of General Maximus's disapproval of him. The Wall is guarded by a motley army, ruffians, thieves, murderers, those sent there as punishment, as well as men of every breed and tongue, the outcasts of civilization, and Parnesius is, at first, miserable. But he finds a friend of wit and energy, Pertinax, and they spend their free time hunting together. They also work together, defending the Wall against the indigenous, rebellious Picts and the invading Vikings. And their years together, laboring in a valiant cause, the defense of their country and its land, make Parnesius and Pertinax happy men.

In "The Winged Hats," we see them as old men. Maximus, who has come to love them for their fidelity, has been captured and executed by his enemies. But the victors know of Parnesius's and Pertinax's long service and offer them a legion in the new army. The two old comrades choose retirement. " 'In War it is as it is in love,' said Pertinax. 'Whether she be good or bad, one gives one's best once, to one only. That given, there remains no second worth giving or taking.' " The quiet end of the two Roman centurions recalls the words of Sir Richard in "Old Men at Pevensey." Una asks him how he spent the time when an old enemy, now a friend, visits him for the last time. "We talked together of times past. That is all men can do when they grow old, little maid."

The rhythms of both the Norman and Roman tales are the same. We meet the characters in their youth and strength. We see them in war and in peace. We watch the development of friendship become a major comfort in life. We watch them decline into old age. These tales all explore the lives of characters who are growing in self-knowledge, who find their best selves in work, especially in defending their land and country. Kipling's love of detail makes vividly different the life of a fourth-century Roman on the Wall from that of an eleventh-century Norman on a Sussex manor; the stories describe landscape, vegetation, climate, dress, speech habits, family patterns. And yet, the virtues celebrated in both periods are the same, boldness, skill, honesty, simplicity, and loyalty. These qualities, as much as the land, are the true inheritance of Dan and Una.

Rewards and Fairies takes up the story, but with a slightly different approach. Again we have Puck and the children; again we see the apparitions from the past. But the tone of these later tales is less ebullient; the major characters are not young men embarking on life's adventures; indeed, characters are not developed, over a series of stories, from youth to old age. The motif that holds these later stories together is rather an attitude toward experience expressed in a refrain that runs through most of them, "what else could I have done?"[19] In "Cold Iron," the young boy who snaps the slave-ring around his neck expresses his reason in those words; constraint and service are his fate. In "A Doctor of Medicine," Nicholas Culpepper enters the plague-ridden town with those words; his duty leaves him no choice. In "Gloriana," Queen Elizabeth appears to the children and discusses the fatal voyage to which she condemned two of her courtiers; their lives had to be sacrificed as a price for peace. She engages Dan and Una in her reasoning. "'D'you think she did right to send 'em?' The lady's voice rose a little. 'Well,' said Dan, 'I don't see what else she could have done.'" For this is a world where labor and devotion may not bring the rewards of success and a peaceful old age. Work, in "Cold Iron," is the slave-ring. An early death awaits the young child in "Mark-lake Witches" as well as Gloriana's courtiers. One's ties to the land are not earned through fruitful labor; often one simply sheds one's blood. This is a world of necessary suffering and sacrifice for the good of others.

Perhaps the quintessential tale in the collection is "The Knife and the Naked Chalk." The children have been taken to the seaside for a month's holiday; they are living "in a flint village on the bare windy chalk Downs." The change in landscape from the lush woods of mid-Sussex to the treeless coastline announces a change to a sterner kind of past that will soon be made available to them. Even Puck, their familiar guide, does not approach them here, but they see him deeply engaged in conversation with a half-naked man who is sharpening a flint arrowhead. And they overhear the conversation. The man, a neolithic shepherd, recounts his struggles to defend himself and his flocks against the Beast, the predatory wolf. His body bears the scars of numerous battles, but he and his people had been helpless against the preying animal. It devoured the sheep at will, even devoured human babies while their parents slept. It was impervious to the arrows shot against it.

The man accidently spies a stranger raising a glistening metal object to defend himself against a wolf. The knife strikes deep into the wolf's heart, and the animal falls dead. The man knows his course; he must secure such knives for his own people. As he travels into the wood to the Children of the Night, a frightening tribe, he knows too that this quest will leave him permanently changed. The Princess of the Children of the Night, after consulting with her gods, agrees to give the man and his people knives. But the gods demand proof of the man's sincerity, of his commitment to his people's welfare. They ask that he sacrifice an eye. And so, the Princess heats a knife and cuts out one of the man's eyes. He returns home with the secret of controlling the Beast and saving his people. They, in return, consider him a god. But such veneration is the second price the man must pay for his gift. Those who once loved him, including a beautiful young maiden, now stand away in awe. He is treated, he says, as if he were dead. In fact, he is no longer part of the living community, but an object set apart.

The man regrets what he has lost; his fate has become a burden not a reward. "And yet," he asks Puck, "what else could I have done?" Knowing the secret that would save his people, he could not refrain from acting on it.

The view of duty, of ties to one's people, of the nature of sacrifice and its consequences is very different here from that developed in the stories about Sir Richard and Sir Hugh. The neolithic man approaches his task with reluctance; he feels no youthful ardor for adventure; he suffers a permanent, pitiful loss; and his triumph becomes merely a means toward future pain. Sir Richard marries the aristocratic Saxon maiden who first disdains him. By his courage and humility, he convinces her of his worthiness. The neolithic man's virtues do not integrate him into a community; they isolate him. Indeed, in *Rewards and Fairies*, developing virtue is often the path to unhappiness. But it is a necessary path for some. "What else could I have done" echoes as the cry of one who sees the right and, willingly or unwillingly, knows he must follow it. Duty in these stories is a stern taskmaster, promising no rewards but self-knowledge. This too is a lesson Dan and Una must learn; the mature and right use of one's gifts may bring no pleasure, but it is an iron duty. Its only reward may be peace of mind, but that brings its own dignity. The story ends as Dan and Una look out on the landscape they once found so forbidding. It has been subtly transformed. "The Downs, that looked so bare and hot when they came, were full of delicious little shadow-dimples; the smell of the thyme and the salt mixed together on the south-west drift from the still sea; their eyes dazzled with the low sun, and the long grass under it looked golden."

The *Just So Stories*, the Jungle Books, and the Puck tales create the magical world of childhood; each in its own way develops a fantastic universe where beauty, power, and mystery mingle, where animals are teachers and guides, or else models of behavior to be shunned, where the visible always has a logical though perhaps unexpected cause, where life's meaning can be made comprehensible without losing its mysterious heart. It is a world where we can learn more than we thought possible, can penetrate to the origin of much that surrounds us, and yet can never fully decipher; we can never enter the mind of the Great Magician. This world never opens its secrets to the scientific, rational mind, the adult mind, but rather to the trusting and the innocent who see with wonder, delight, and awe.

The allegorical component of these tales changes from book to book, in some stories more discernible than in others, but it never overwhelms the narrative or reduces it to a preordained pattern of meanings. The stories retain a playfulness, a delight in individual characters and a good plot, a dramatic energy, an emotional intensity, and a joy in lush visual description that surpass intellectual symmetry.

These tales approach the concerns of childhood in different ways. The *Just So Stories* are a series of disparate tales built around a clever idea. The Mowgli stories are a profoundly imaginative and moral exploration of human growth and development. We witness the dangers that surround the child, and yet the sense of safety and reassurance that come from knowing we are protected by those who love us. Finally, Mowgli becomes more powerful than his protectors and must leave them behind, taking their lessons into a world that often does not recognize their value. Mowgli's ambivalence about reentering the human world has been prepared for throughout the stories and gives a slight autumnal note to even the most ebullient of them.

We do not witness the development of Dan and Una in the same way. We hear with them the stories from the past and Puck's dialogues with their visitors; we deduce the lessons the children are expected to take away from these encounters, but we do not see Dan and Una grow up or change. Still, these are books that imply a satisfying adulthood for these children in a way the Jungle Books do not. While Mowgli's integration into the human world must be felt as a diminishment, Dan and Una's is seen as an enrichment. The Puck books presuppose the unity of human experience; people in the past were like us, and we can learn from them, applying their wisdom to our own lives. History is both cumulative and cyclical.[20]

On the surface, these fantastic tales seem very different from Kipling's other work. They do not give us the sharp, satirical voice of the Anglo-Indian tales, the realistic treatment of social intercourse or psychic torment. They lack the rich and shifting perspectives of a sharply defined narrative voice, the mix of sympathy and irony. They are closer in tone perhaps to Kipling's idealistic treatments of Empire, such as "William the Conqueror." But they do embody values that are familiar: a belief in law, in the strength that community provides, in the importance of work as a contribution to the general good and a stabilizing force in one's own life, in the iron command of duty and sometimes of sacrifice. The stoic vision that underlies Kipling's view of

Empire is iterated in the Law of the Jungle and in the lives of the Roman centurions and Norman conquerors.

But there are a handful of new motifs in these tales, ideas that may have been touched on earlier but were latent until these children's books. The deep love of the English landscape, so apparent in the Puck books, is given wider treatment in Kipling's later work; so, too, is the belief that the English are inheritors of a tradition that will outlast the individual. But even more central to Kipling's development is his treatment here of aged characters who live on after disappointment or catastrophe. Sir Richard and Parnesius, enduring their lives after their duty is over, after the death of those they loved, after their energy has been spent, are characters who point us forward in two ways, in their fate and in the mysterious sources of their fidelity to life when its ostensible meanings have been taken away. Even within his children's books, in fantasy and allegory, Kipling still strikes to the heart of the lonely human condition, a concern, though changing in fictional presentation, that never diminishes in his work.

Enigmas and Mysteries

The mythic worlds of Kipling's children's stories demonstrate his interest in portraying life as something that does not yield its secrets to the operations of mere intellect. The fairy-tale quality of these stories, and the fact that they were originally addressed to children, demand for their enjoyment that the reader accept the fantastic as a condition of life. But in many stories that do not partake of an overarching imaginary world, indeed that purport to be realistic, that treat the lives of civil servants in India, sailors stationed in New Zealand, or working-class widows in English suburbs, Kipling still enjoys exploring the mysterious. In his brief preface to the first edition of *The Phantom 'Rickshaw and Other Tales,* Kipling writes, "this is not exactly a book of real ghost-stories, as the cover [a macabre sketch by Kipling's father] makes believe, but rather a collection of facts that never quite explained themselves."[21]

Such unexplained facts are a recurring topic from the earliest to the latest stories. They may be small-scale enigmatic events and their effects may be humorous, or they may adumbrate some of the more profound aspects of human experience, finally encompassing a mode of apprehension one might call religious. And, just as in his children's stories, where Kipling depicts a closely detailed natural world in service to his imaginative vision, so, in these stories dealing with mysteries, he embeds his explorations of the unknown in a narrative filled with specific, quotidian details, the minutiae of daily life in an Anglo-Indian station or the intricacies of repairing a motor car. Yet, the true focus of this large group of Kipling's stories is the event whose cause is unknowable or irrational. The narrator, awed or mystified or shaken, looks on a world he can describe but cannot comprehend, and the reader is left to make what sense he or she can of the story.

In the Anglo-Indian tales, the narrator's perplexity may be a consequence of the difference between the Eastern and Western minds; what the West dismisses as superstition may emerge as potent reality. As Kipling suggests, one recurrent form in the Anglo-Indian tales is the ghost story. He often has his narrator introduce the tale, unsure of what to make of his material yet eager to relate it, knowing his reader will be skeptical but convinced the story he tells is true. "My Own True Ghost Story" (*PR*) is as much a study in circumstance and atmosphere as an anecdote about a ghost. Indeed, one might say its true subject is the wretched life of an obscure Anglo-Indian civil servant, amidst duties he despises and conditions he cannot control. Traveling from one remote station to another, greeted only by the obligatory Indian servant, he is alone in the vast Indian landscape.

The narrator begins by discussing the many different kinds of ghosts one can encounter in India and remarks superciliously that no Englishman can be frightened by a native ghost, though English ghosts can terrify the English and natives alike. His story demonstrates this generalization, as the young official, stopping overnight in a government-provided bungalow, hears a game of billiards being played in the room next to his. Knowing no one else is there to play, indeed the room is too small to contain a billiard table, he learns the next morning that in years past, before the large room was subdivided, a billiard table occupied the space and was frequently used by the English. He has been hearing the game of long-dead railway workers.

Although the narrator vividly describes the near panic he felt lying in his bed overhearing the ghostly game, once he learns the identity of the spirits, his fears are relieved. Indeed, he walks about the billiard room the next morning, listening to another game being played. His only regret, finally, is that because the spirits soon cease their noise, he will never be able to provide evidence for the story he intends to tell of them. The hardships of the Englishman's life in India, the confrontation with another dimension of existence, concerns with which the story begins, all dissipate in the cool nonchalance of the self-satisfied narrator who has solved the puzzle of his unseen visitors. The reader's task, however, is not so much to pinpoint the source of the ghosts as to account for the mood of the tale, a dispassionate recounting of terror and an easy ability to forget it.

But the very offhandedness of the narrator's response to the ghosts suggests something of the familiarity of such visitations in India and the attitude the Anglo-Indian must adopt if he is to carry on his daily life. In "Haunted Subalterns" (*PTH*), Tesser, the young junior officer, is tormented by a "Devil," an invisible force that enters and ransacks his room when he is away, that proceeds to play his banjo so loudly everyone in the cantonment can hear it. But no one can see the Devil except Tesser's Indian bearer. And finally Tesser is forced to leave for the hill country to escape his tormenter. No rational explanation is offered the reader for all this. On the contrary, the narrator explicitly refuses one. "If I had invented this story," he concludes, "I should have put in a satisfactory ending." But he does not choose between two explanations, a practical joke and an otherworldly apparition. He ends the story, "you must settle that for yourselves."

The story's narrator is not its protagonist, but an unspecified reporter who demonstrates a knowledge of the men and milieu he describes, the familiar voice Kipling creates in many of these tales, close enough to the Anglo-Indian community to know its ways and yet possessing a bemused distance. The two stories acknowledge those aspects of Indian life that baffle the English mind while portraying the disparaging attitude Kipling's characters often use as a defense. The tales do not explore those states of mind or the ghosts that occasion them. Kipling draws his readers into this complex world and leaves them there, almost as if they were part of a large practical joke they cannot understand.

These slight stories seem to locate the perplexing in the Indian world; the Anglo-Indian becomes the obtuse but innocent victim of an unseen power. But Kipling has a large group of tales in which the mysterious affects those who, because of their behavior, incur its animosity. "The Mark of the Beast" (*LH*) begins with the narrator's statement of the incommensurability of the Eastern and Western systems of values, particularly religious values. "East of Suez, some hold, the direct control of Providence ceases; Man being there handed over to the power of the Gods and Devils of Asia, and the Church of England Providence only exercising an occasional and modified supervision in the case of Englishmen." But, as the tale progresses, this neat demarcation between East and West is muddied.

Fleete, a newcomer to India, is spending his holidays in the station. After a hard-drinking New Year's Eve party, Fleete storms into the temple of Hanuman, the Monkey-god, and pollutes the sacred space by touching the priests and grinding his cigar ashes into the statue of the divinity. The police chief, Strickland, and the narrator, both experienced Anglo-Indians, are horrified by Fleete's behavior and drag him home, but not before a Silver Man, a leper who inhabits the temple, grasps Fleete and lays his head on the drunken man's breast. The rest of the tale recounts Fleete's transformation into a wild animal, snarling, howling, crawling in the dirt, eating raw meat. Strickland and the narrator, at last realizing what has occurred, torture the leper until he releases Fleete from the curse.

Repeatedly throughout the tale, the narrator draws his original distinction between East and West. Fleete has gotten himself mixed up with an Eastern god and is suffering a vicious retribution. And by torturing the leper, Strickland and the narrator believe they have put aside Western values and entered an Eastern pattern of behavior; "we had fought for Fleete's soul with the Silver Man in that room, and had disgraced ourselves as Englishmen for ever."

But the reader may not be as willing to draw these distinctions. Fleete has acted in a way that would bring down the wrath of believers of any religion. He, the pugnacious outsider, with contempt for the spiritual values of his host country, has defiled a sacred object. The Silver Man's response, his anger and his desire to punish Fleete, are understandable. The form that response takes is, to be sure, incomprehensible to our ordinary mind; the Westerner cannot bestialize another. And yet, perhaps, the Silver Man has merely given a pattern of behavior to the spirit Fleete has already demonstrated; he has materialized Fleete's soul. Almost like a Dantean figure, Fleete, as punishment, must perform the physical acts that symbolize his spiritual transgression.

Strickland and the narrator are able to release Fleete, who emerges with no memory of his act or its consequences. But the reader is left to ponder Fleete's fate and, at the same time, to question the narrator's interpretation. This is not entirely a story about the difference between Eastern and Western gods. And the narrator admits he cannot "clear up the mystery" of what happened to Fleete. He ironically repeats conventional Western wisdom; "it is well known to every right-minded man that the Gods of the heathen are stone and brass, and any attempt to deal with them otherwise is justly condemned." But he has already rejected this view, though having nothing to substitute for it. The reader, who has been led into the mystery with the narrator, who has seen no farther into the story than the narrator, who has no other answer than the narrator's confusion, yet views Fleete's experience in larger, more universal terms than the narrator can admit. More than an anecdote about the power of Eastern religion, this is a story about how human beings, through self-indulgence, ignorance, and aggression, turn themselves into brutes. Fleete, however, has learned nothing from his experience. And the narrator remains perplexed.

In "The Mark of the Beast" we move out of the realm of the simple ghost story into a world where mysterious consequences derive, at least in part, from characters' values and behavior. We may not fully understand the causes of events but we can see their appropriateness. And the irrational becomes less a function of cultural dislocation and more a confrontation with a hitherto unrecognized aspect of one's character. Kipling has many characters who undergo a mysterious but fitting fate. One thinks of Morrowbie Jukes, whose fall into the land of the living dead is his initiation into the underside of the Anglo-Indian world that has supported him.

One of Kipling's earliest stories, "The Phantom 'Rickshaw" (*PR*), is one of his most successful explorations of a character whose unacknowledged guilt forces itself into his consciousness in a dreadful and unearthly way. One of Kipling's typical unnamed narrators introduces the story of Jack Pansay, whose illness and death are attributed by the physician, Heatherlegh, to overwork. The narrator has another theory; "there was a crack in Pansay's head and a little bit of the Dark World came through and pressed him to death." Most of the tale is Pansay's own detailed narration, written on his deathbed. A few years earlier, Pansay, a civil servant, had begun a love affair with a married woman, Agnes Keith-Wessington. Pansay soon tired of Agnes and told her so in unnecessarily cruel terms. "From my own lips, in August 1882, she learnt that I was sick of her presence, tired of her company, and weary of the sound of her voice." But Mrs. Wessington does not accept this rejection. She continues to put herself in Pansay's path at every opportunity, vowing they will be reunited. Pansay becomes more brutal with each encounter. "My answer might have made even a man wince. It cut the dying woman before me like the blow of a whip." And Agnes does die, though not before Pansay has told her he is engaged to marry another.

Pansay's sadism toward Agnes is answered by her increasing pleading and cringing. Their relationship becomes one of torment; he, the powerful, seems to take a ghastly pleasure in hurting her, while she seems able only to intensify her self-abasement. Pansay has an occasional twinge of conscience; "Mrs. Wessington broke down completely. I turned away and left her to finish her journey in peace, feeling, but only for a moment or two, that I had been an unutterably mean hound." But he pushes this feeling aside as he delights in his bride-to-be.

Mrs. Wessington has pursued Pansay from her yellow-paneled rickshaw, drawn by her servants, her *jhampanies*, in their black and white livery. Eight months after her death, however, Pansay again sees Mrs. Wessington's rickshaw and livery. At first he thinks someone has purchased her effects. But he discovers not only that others cannot see his apparition, but that they can walk right through it when it appears on the road. Soon Agnes herself inhabits the rickshaw and begins following Pansay everywhere, still pleading for a reconciliation. He stops, terrified, whenever he sees her carriage in the road. Gradually, Pansay's friends begin to fear for his sanity, and he, in his desire to explain his vision, blurts out his shameful treatment of Mrs. Wessington. His former cruelty and present hallucinations combine to drive his friends and fiancée away in disgust. Finally, Pansay is drawn back to the only one who unconditionally accepts him, Mrs. Wessington. He walks the streets of Simla, accompanying her rickshaw, the two deep in conversation, feeling, he says, as if he is wooing her again. The two become the only reality to him; all else is shadow. And Pansay acknowledges his responsibility for Mrs. Wessington's death. He knows he is dying and about to join her, and their daily walks become both a penance and a source of strange contentment.

Pansay never fully understands what has happened to him; he describes his "sensation of dull, numbing wonder that the seen and the Unseen should mingle so strangely on this earth to hound one poor soul to its grave." Although he accepts the fitness of his haunting, he cannot explain it. And the story ends with Pansay baffled and dying, admitting his guilt yet powerless to assuage it. Mrs. Wessington, in her way, is even less merciful than Pansay was to her, or perhaps Pansay is incapable of forgiving himself. Though the narrative never rejects the possibility that Agnes is an otherworldly visitor, the story dwells more fully on Pansay's guilt, so profound and, at first, unacknowledged that the sufferer gives a body and action to his repressed emotion, literally confronts the specter of his conscience. The story leaves the reader poised between two worlds, the supernatural and the psychological, the terms in which the experience presents itself and the state that propels the experience. It is a place where many of Kipling's enigmatic stories exist.

A later story, "The Brushwood Boy" (*DW*), focuses on the intersection between dream and reality. Young George Cottar, whom we watch develop from a child to the youngest major in the Indian Army, finds his greatest reality not in his work or family but in his dream life.

From the age of six he has developed an elaborate dream, consisting of a series of heroic adventures, accompanied by a girl who matures into a beautiful young woman, occurring in a fantastic geographical space detailed enough for him to map. At the end of the story, George is introduced to a family friend, the young woman who inhabits his dreams. In a song she has composed and sings, George recognizes his dream landscape; in fact, the girl has from childhood had the same dreams as George. They instantly acknowledge that an inexplicable fate has drawn them together by providing them with a shared consciousness. The story ends when, eight hours after they meet, they decide to marry, worried only about how they will preserve propriety, mimic a courtship, until they can wed. They feel no need of any further knowledge of each other than they already have. They have lived within each other's deepest consciousness for so long that they already feel as one.

The story attempts no explanation of George and Miriam's situation, and it is presented as a happy gift to two deserving and remarkable young people. But Kipling more often treats the inexplicable, as in "The Phantom 'Rickshaw," as a sign of a troubled conscience or the arena for working out an acknowledged or unacknowledged guilt.

One of Kipling's most opaque stories, and certainly one that has occasioned an extensive critical commentary, is "Mrs Bathurst."[22] If his enigmatic tales often involve a problematic narrator, one who does not understand the full meaning of what he is relating, Kipling takes this form a step further in this tale. Here the reader must piece together the information and responses of four narrators, none of whom knows the full story. Indeed the very process of ascertaining simple facts and, what may be more difficult, their significance is a central concern of the story. The narrator and Hooper, old acquaintances waiting at a railroad siding outside Cape Town, encounter Pyecroft and Pritchard, two seamen, the former an old friend of the narrator's. These four men share a few bottles of ale, and, from the very beginning of the story, the reader is forced to sort out the bits of anecdotes the men provide. They speak of others they have known, adventures they have had, but one man may begin a story and another finish it, or one story may be interrupted and never completed. Characters in the anecdotes are never fully identified. The structure of this frame is associative, accidental, and allusive.

As the story progresses, the men begin to concentrate on the central anecdote, the story of Mrs. Bathurst and Vickery, the seamen's friend.

But even here no one knows the full story; one man may know of some episodes; another may know of some gossip; a third may, unbeknownst to him until now, have been a witness to a possible conclusion to the story, but it takes all four men, sitting together, each contributing a detail or fact, like pieces in a jigsaw puzzle, to put it all together. Even then, after everyone has made his contribution, no one is quite sure of the facts; certainly, no one fully knows what to make of them.

A few things seem certain. Mrs. Bathurst, a widow, kept a small hotel near Auckland, New Zealand, an establishment frequented largely by sailors on leave. Generous and warm-hearted, Mrs. Bathurst was respected and admired by her customers. But she also possessed a charismatic quality that drew others to her and made her unforgettable. Pyecroft explains, " 'tisn't beauty, so to speak, nor good talk necessarily. It's just It. Some women 'll stay in a man's memory if they once walk down a street." Pyecroft meets Vickery on a voyage. And they come ashore together in Cape Town, South Africa, where the cinematograph is the new sensation. Vickery talks Pyecroft into accompanying him, and, for four nights in a row, they return to watch a forty-five-second film of a train arriving at Paddington Station and a woman disembarking, carrying a bag and walking toward the camera until she disappears from the frame. Pyecroft, Vickery, and another old Auckland cohort all recognize the woman as Mrs. Bathurst. But her reason for traveling to England, her experience there, her fate, even the particular time when this scene occurred, are all unknown to the friends. But Vickery is obsessed. Each night he watches the film and then drags Pyecroft from bar to bar until they fall into drunken oblivion. Pyecroft questions Vickery only once, " 'I wonder what she's doin' in England,' I says. 'Don't it seem to you she's lookin' for somebody?' " "She's lookin' for me," replies Vickery.

Drawn back night after night to this image of Mrs. Bathurst, Vickery is driven to such distraction that he deserts the navy and takes off on his own. At the end of the story, Hooper, who has never heard of Vickery before, reveals he had recently been called in to investigate two tramps walking through a forest toward the Zambesi River in Africa. By the time he arrived, they were dead; apparently struck by lightning, their bodies had been burnt to charcoal. But some idiosyncratic false teeth and a pattern of tattoos still visible suggest one of the tramps was Vickery.

The story draws no conclusions from all this. Vickery speaks defensively at one point about not being a murderer; his wife, he says, died a natural death in childbirth. But why he should fear being suspected of murder is not made clear. Vickery seems one of those characters driven by some kind of guilt and haunted by a ghost, here not a hallucination but the flickering image of a woman he had once known who, he is convinced, has been searching for him. Before he dies, Vickery has started on his own search; neither the narrator nor the reader ever knows toward what goal.

"Mrs Bathurst" is a tale that opens up only to reveal deeper and deeper mysteries. The reader has difficulty understanding the narrators; they do not fully understand each other. In fact, they quarrel and correct each other. Pyecroft does not understand Vickery's obsession. Vickery, at the cinema, does not know the fate of the pursuing Mrs. Bathurst, perhaps does not even know she had been seeking him. Mrs. Bathurst, herself, does not seem to know the whereabouts of the man. The reader is not even sure that her trip was a search. A conundrum of hints, misperceptions, incomplete information, guilt, and suffering, the story suggests answers but provides none. Many different readings are possible. Vickery, in love with Mrs. Bathurst, may have urged her to join him in London, even though he already had a wife there. Her appearance at Paddington Station would then suggest she did follow him, perhaps only to learn of his wife. Or she may have sought him out without his knowing she did so. Vickery may have left his ship to seek Mrs. Bathurst or simply to lose himself. Mrs. Bathurst may be the second tramp struck by lightning, or may not. The cinematographic image of Mrs. Bathurst becomes an emblem of the tale, an illusion adumbrating a mystery.

But one thing is certain: the hidden motives of Mrs. Bathurst and Vickery drive her into oblivion and him to death. In many stories treating the incomprehensible, characters suffer from their obsessive desires, either because of guilt or because the unconsuming flame of the desire itself drives them toward annihilation. "A Madonna of the Trenches" and "Uncovenanted Mercies" (*L&R*) provide ready examples. But Kipling has another group of stories, which become more numerous as he grows older, that treat the mysterious as a source of joy, healing, or reconciliation. "The Brushwood Boy" is an early example of this. "The House Surgeon" (*A&R*) is more typical of Kipling's later work; here the mysterious is a source of pain that can be mysteriously alleviated. The story bears some resemblances to Kipling's ghost stories. The narrator, humorously dubbed Perseus by his new friends, is invited to visit the elegant country house of the M'Leods; Perseus has just met Mr. M'Leod, who recounts the devastating depression that settles over the house periodically, a black pall that covers the spirits of its inhabitants, driving them to despair and thoughts of suicide. After spending a weekend with the M'Leods and experiencing the misery the family must regularly endure, Perseus takes up the challenge of discovering its source. After ingratiating himself with the solicitor who handled the sale of the house to the M'Leods, Perseus learns that a former owner is thought to have committed suicide while living there. The dead Agnes has never been forgiven by her sister Mary for having committed this sinful act. It is Mary's animosity and the unhappy presence of Agnes yearning to tell the truth about her death that have infected the house. Perseus brings Mary back to Agnes's room to show how, in fact, the death was an accident, a fall from an upstairs window located too close to the floor. The merest stumble toward that window could result in a fatal fall. Mary has almost fallen from a similar window and recognizes the likelihood of her sister's death as being accidental. The misery that has pervaded the house departs as the two sisters, one living and one dead, are reconciled to each other.

Evil in this tale is discovered to be illusory, a mistake; once the truth is uncovered, the misery recedes. Characters are not punished for their sins; they punish themselves and are harsher than any outside judge would be. Indeed, the solicitor had been in love with Agnes when they were young, but she refused him, unwilling to leave her sisters. He has long ago forgiven the pain the family caused him and remains a faithful visitor to the two living sisters. " 'People ought to forgive and forget,' he volunteered one day between rounds [of a golf game]. 'Specially where, in the nature of things, they can't be sure of their deductions.' " Being sure of one's deductions takes on a larger meaning; that human beings never fully understand the minds of others is a familiar motif in Kipling's stories, and, if in the early tales this is something that cannot be helped, is simply a human fact, in many later stories it is a reason for forgiveness and charity.

Still, in "The House Surgeon," these themes are embedded in a narrative that is part ghost story and part detective story. And the answer to the puzzle of the house's haunting is the mysterious psychic energies that emanate from both the living and the dead. In "The

Miracle of Saint Jubanus" (*L&R*) Kipling deals with another condition that occurs often in his late work, shell shock. And, like "A Madonna of the Trenches," which examines Strangwick's neurosis and finds its cause in the mysterious suicide pact between his dying aunt and her lover, "The Miracle of Saint Jubanus" deals with love and the other-worldly, but in a light, humorous tone, where we cannot fully distinguish between saintly intervention and ludicrous confusion.

The tale recounts the healing of young Martin, a World War I veteran, of the silence and despair that have overtaken him since his return from the front. The curé of the tiny country church tells the narrator of his prayer to St. Jubanus, the local patron saint. He also speaks of Falloux, the village atheist, the curé's friend and partner at cards. Martin's spirit is restored, that is, he laughs out loud in delight, when the rough-edged spokes of the curé's recently repaired umbrella catch onto the clothes of first one and then a second acolyte. The children cannot break free, and Falloux attempts to help them. He merely catches his own beard in the umbrella. The three prisoners of the open umbrella find themselves in a bizarre dance through the sanctuary as they push and pull against each other trying to extricate themselves from the umbrella that seems to have taken on a life of its own; "my insolent umbrella promenaded its three adherents through pagan undulations and genuflexions. It was Salome's basin, you understand, dancing by itself with every appearance of enjoyment, and offering to all quarters the head of the Apostles *and* two of the Innocents." The scriptural vocabulary continues. After Martin laughs, "tears from the soul," the curé tells him and his girlfriend to walk away from the Mass about to begin, "go out, my children. All the world is for you today Paradise. Enter there."

Their joy is their taste of Paradise. But the story takes the "miracle" a step further. The saint values forgiveness and mercy. The curé believes he has triumphed over his old antagonist, Falloux, by having the atheist appear a fool. But the saint works his power on the curé, makes him pity Falloux, wanting to save the old man's dignity. The curé announces to the congregation that Falloux has willingly participated in the farce to help heal Martin. There is a rational explanation for the umbrella's actions, of course; its ragged spokes easily catch onto fibers. But the curé does not accept that. He believes his prayer to Saint Jubanus was answered, and in a particularly Jubanian manner, for the saint is associated with his sense of humor, "something of a *farceur*," says the curé. But the story remains mute on the choice of causes. Still, the effects of the "miracle" are clear enough, healing, laughter, forgiveness, mercy, and love, all of which well accord with the beneficent concerns of the saint.

Such interest in mysterious psychic phenomena and miracles persists into Kipling's last stories. But the unmitigated delight of "The Miracle of Saint Jubanus" and the happy resolution of "The House Surgeon" are not the typical moods in the late tales. On the contrary, the last stories eke out their joy in the face of difficult and painful circumstances; often the unhappiness is so palpable, the joy seems a hard-earned rebuke to the general tenor of life. Many commentators on Kipling's work have noted the sadness at the heart of his last stories; they attribute it to the difficulties of old age; failing health; increasing pain from an undiagnosed ulcer; the deaths of two of his three children, six-year-old Josephine in 1899, and his only son, John, missing in action in 1915. Though the narratives in the late stories focus still on the puzzling or inexplicable, their ambiguities become absorbed into a religious perspective.

"Uncovenanted Mercies" takes place in heaven and hell as Gabriel, Satan, the Angel of Death, and the Angel of the English discuss their work in guiding, testing, and redeeming human souls. The story explores the importance of fidelity between those who love and the forces that act to undermine such loyalty. Two human beings, whom the angelic forces had hoped to keep apart forever, accidentally meet and fall in love. Lifelong circumstances prevent their union, but they vow to be faithful and, when released from their earthly obligations, to meet again on Judgment Day. They are put to the "full test for Ultimate Breaking Strain," each led to believe the other has not kept the vow, but both remain constant, unwilling to believe the worst, determined to wait even after death for the other. No evil the universe can work is strong enough to defeat their love, and even Satan takes pity and allows their reconciliation.

Although the story takes place in the supernatural realm, it is almost mundane in its treatment of its characters. It does not explore subtle mental states or even the particular bond that holds the couple together. The setting may be unrealistic, but Kipling treats the events in a matter-of-fact tone.

More interesting and much more evocative is " 'They' " (*T&D*), the narrative of a middle-aged man who, while enjoying a ride in that newfangled invention, the motor car, loses his way in the Sussex countryside and comes upon the house and grounds of a beautiful Elizabethan manor. The story is rich in painterly detail of countryside, garden, and house, of the shifting lights of late afternoon and early eve-ning, of the changing colors from spring through summer to autumn. The man makes three trips to the house, learning more of the life of its blind mistress and the children she cares for. He never fully sees the children, but catches glimpses of them as they peep out from behind the shrubbery or hide behind doors. He hears their footsteps and soft laughter and feels the profound peace that inhabits the scene.

The story plays with seeing and blindness. The narrator is at first captured by the visual splendor of the scene and is delicate and precise in his description. But although he very much wants to see the children, they hide from him out of shyness; he has the physiological ability to see them but is not permitted to do so. Miss Florence, their guardian, blind from infancy, dwells in their presence, has their confidence, but is incapable of seeing them. Through his friendship with Miss Florence and his kindness to the people of the nearby village when they are in distress, the narrator is allowed to penetrate deeper into the house and its mystery until, finally, he crosses the threshold that separates him from the children. As he sits in an armchair with his hand hanging loosely, a small mouth plants a gentle kiss on his palm. He immediately recognizes the gift; such a touch was a silent signal of affection between him and his now-dead young daughter. The children so lovingly cared for in this house are all dead. It is only because Miss Florence was so lonely and so longed for children that she has been granted the gift of caring for these gentle, needy souls. Though the narrator can feel his child's presence, he can never see her. And he knows he must never return. For one moment, he has been blessed by the kiss of his beloved child; for one moment he has felt complete happiness. But he cannot enter the world of the dead. For one reason or another, that world remains close enough to touch but just forever out of sight. And the narrator accepts his fate; he returns to his motor car and his old life, the world of flesh, not of spirit.

The story mingles the physical and the spiritual, presence and vanishings. Kipling gives an intense physicality to this shimmering, otherworldly house of the dead. The tone of the tale, a gentle sorrow mixed with a gentle joy, demonstrates the belief prevalent in many of the late tales: the spiritual life, where love dwells, may be more powerful and more meaningful than the mundane, but we have not the ability to choose one and reject the other. We must go back to our daily lives and take up our burdens; these burdens may be eased by love and faith, but are still inescapable. Kipling heightens the poignancy of the father's fate by having him serve as the solitary narrator of his own tale. So many of Kipling's stories work through complex shifts of perspective and voice, calling into question the central narrative event and its meaning. But here the character's emotions are seemingly unmediated by art; they speak to the reader in an acute simplicity.

The elegiac quality of this story, often thought a memorial to Kipling's daughter, is evident too in "The Gardener" (*D&C*), often thought a memorial to his son. As in " 'They,' " the narrative strategy in "The Gardener" is crucial. Although " 'They' " contains many suggestions that Miss Florence's home is mysterious, we learn the full truth only when the narrator does. "The Gardener" has an omniscient narrator who provides the information necessary for our full understanding, but in so subtle and ironic a manner that we may not know how to interpret the story until the final scene. We never know if the central character fully realizes what has occurred. One cannot fully appreciate Kipling's control in a first reading.

The story tells of Helen Turrell's taking upon herself the responsibility for the rearing of the young child left behind in France when her brother dies. The child's mother, Helen has told her friends, readily relinquished him, and Helen returns to her small English village with her infant nephew, Michael. We watch her affection for the child grow and watch Michael's love for Helen develop. The young man enlists in the army and is killed in France. Toward the end of the story Helen makes a pilgrimage to his grave. Overwhelmed by the sea of black crosses, unable to locate the grave number she has been given, she turns in distress to a man tending some plants. The story's tone, delicate and simple yet suffused with sadness, comes to a climax in their exchange. "He rose at her approach and without prelude or salutation asked: 'Who are you looking for?' 'Lieutenant Michael Turrell—my nephew,' said Helen slowly and word for word, as she had many thousands of times in her life. The man lifted his eyes and looked at her with infinite compassion before he turned from the fresh-sown grass toward the naked black crosses. 'Come with me' he said, 'and I will show you where your son lies.' "

As the reader suddenly realizes, Helen's life has been a camouflage; Michael had been her illegitimate son. And the intense love they shared was made unnecessarily painful because its true source had never been revealed. Helen tried all her life to allow Michael the experience of a natural loving family without ever acknowledging that they, in fact, were exactly that. But how much anyone else knew of the truth is left ambiguous. The story's opening words at first seem straightforward: "everyone in the village knew" Helen was doing her duty by her nephew. But the phrase takes on a different implication after one has finished the tale. Helen's secret may well have been common knowledge and only the respect of her neighbors allowed her the dignity of preserving her lie.

In her conversation in the cemetery, her secret burden is lifted for a moment and she is permitted the honor and grief that belong to her as Michael's mother. For her to achieve that moment of honesty requires divine intervention. She leaves the cemetery, glancing back at the man, "supposing him to be the gardener." Helen's situation and Kipling's language both echo the description in John 20:15 of Mary Magdalene's seeking Jesus' tomb, only to find it empty. Jesus appears to her and asks "whom seekest thou?" She, "supposing him to be the gardener," asks in fear if he knows where the body is. The fallen woman, seeking the body of one she loves, the Christ who eases her pain, her ignorance of his identity are all vividly re-created in the story. Helen moves into the world of Christian comfort for a moment, but then reenters daily reality. For she will return to her village to take up her old life. Yet, her pain has been acknowledged for a moment by another's recognition of the truth. Kipling's narrative keeps Helen's secret for her until the gardener's remark. We never enter her mind to see her complex responses to Michael or to the lies she fosters in the village. She remains elusive, and even her visit to the grave is left undescribed. The narrator, in reporting Helen's conversation with the gardener, makes the facts of her life clear, but her experience of those facts remains hidden from us. Moreover, she never realizes the identity of her guide.

Kipling explores another kind of pain, another kind of release, and another narrative approach to the mysterious in "The Wish House" (*D&C*). This tale also treats love as a means of crossing the threshold between the natural and supernatural. But if the father in " 'They' " and Helen Turrell touch a mysterious reconciling power yet must return finally to their daily lives, in "The Wish House" the central character, Grace Ashcroft, bears forever on her flesh the ineradicable mark of the mysterious power of love. It has been a source of recurring pain and will soon lead to her death.

Mrs. Ashcroft, an elderly working-class widow, now living out the end of a hard life, is spending an afternoon with an old friend, Liz

85

Fettley, who has traveled thirty miles by bus for a few hours of chat and tea. The two old women reminisce about their youth, exchanging stories of lovers and escapades. Mrs. Ashcroft freely admits her promiscuity, even when married. But she dwells most on her one great love, Harry Mockler, a man who soon grew tired of her. Her love for him was so profound, however, that Mrs. Ashcroft could face even his coolness as long as he was happy. But it becomes apparent that Harry is ill; he grows thin and is clearly in pain.

A young child who had taken a fancy to Mrs. Aschroft, following her, cuddling her when she is at rest, is able finally to assume the debilitating pain of one of Mrs. Ashcroft's headaches. The child, Sophy, reveals the existence of a wish house, an abandoned building that yet seems mysteriously inhabited. One can approach and whisper a wish through the letter box, but only one kind of wish is allowed, to take upon oneself someone else's trouble. After much thought, Mrs. Ashcroft walks to the house and asks, "let me take everythin' bad that's in store for my man, 'Arry Mockler, for love's sake." Soon afterward, Mrs. Ashcroft injures her leg and develops an open, running sore that never heals. Harry Mockler soon recovers from his wasting disease, but Mrs. Ashcroft's leg becomes a permanent source of pain. At times the pain subsides, but when Harry is in need, it returns. And her pain becomes her link with Harry. Though he may be far away, she knows the rhythm of his life, for she feels it in her body. And the sweetest part of her reward is that Harry knows nothing of all this. Not only has his body been spared suffering, his mind has been spared an incomparable gratitude. He simply lives out his charmed life. But Mrs. Ashcroft has had one particular consolation; she has not had to watch Harry marry another; his mother, a harridan, frightens all other women away. This is Mrs. Ashcroft's reward. Her pains, she says, have averted that disaster.

But Mrs. Ashcroft's final question to Mrs. Fettley reveals her fears, "the pain *do* count, don't ye think, Liz?" The pain has counted to keep Harry happy, to keep her the secret provider; now, on her deathbed, she asks no other reward than that her lifelong pain act as a testament to her love.

Mrs. Ashcroft may seem an unlikely character for a story that explores the redemptive power of love and locates its effectiveness in the mysterious, irrational wish house. For this uneducated, hard-working, pragmatic, sexual being, often selfish and unfaithful, emerges as an agent of a love so powerful it heals and saves another. The Christian imagery of "The Gardener" is absent here, but the Christian tradition of sacrificial love is central; Grace Ashcroft, whose first name indicates her role, gives her life for Harry and does so joyfully.

Yet the story never diminishes the cost of her sacrifice. The physical ugliness of her sore, her intractable pain, as well as the poverty and loneliness of her life, are made real. Typical of Kipling's mingling of precise physical detail and mysterious meaning, "The Wish House" sees the greatest mystery as that of love and this great power as one that exists in the most humble of circumstances. And here Kipling merges the immediacy of the central character's speaking voice with the perspective of an omniscient narrator. We learn Mrs. Ashcroft's story from her own lips, a report of her conversation with Mrs. Fettley. But the incongruity between her humble circumstances and the heroic power of her love is provided by the narrator's detailed description of her lower-middle-class council house existence. This tale of a magical house and the assumption of another's pain is rooted in precise quotidian detail.

From his earliest works, from the Anglo-Indian ghost stories, to his last, and with an astonishing variety of narrative strategies, Kipling demonstrated an interest in those aspects of life that escape our rational powers. They may be labeled superstition or guilt; they may seem to find their origin outside or inside the self. They may cause fear or pain or a bittersweet joy. But they are an undeniable part of human existence. The mind cannot comprehend all; at times in Kipling's work, it seems as if the rational mind can understand very little of importance. In his early work, some characters react to this with fear, some with panic, and some with denial. But in his last stories, characters who have devoted their lives to the good of another accept the mystery at the heart of life, step into it in search of love and peace, and find that it heals and saves.

Kipling the Artist

For so prolific a writer as Kipling, one who treats in his work so many matters of serious human import with a craftsmanship that demonstrates both assurance and dazzling variety, relatively little attention has been paid to elements of style, to overt or implicit references to art. Kipling himself is of course somewhat to blame. He was persistently reluctant to discuss his work and, when pressed by circumstances to do so, often employed allegory or metaphor to create a fable of the artist.[23] In his autobiography, *Something of Myself,* Kipling devotes a chapter to his work, "Tools of My Trade." In editing the manuscript for publication after her husband's death, Caroline Kipling changed the title to "Working Tools" (260, n1), but the focus remains; Kipling treats art almost as if it were a manual skill, as if writing were largely a matter of good paper and proper ink. Kipling's other major image for artistic creation is his "Daemon," the force that inspires him. He repeatedly invokes the Daemon to explain his choice of subjects, his development of plot and character, the energy of a piece of writing. He makes himself seem almost an empty vessel. "When your Daemon is in charge," he writes in *Something of Myself,* "do not try to think consciously. Drift, wait, and obey" (123).

Dividing his discussions of his art in this way, allocating his creativity to an outside force and the polish of his expression to his craftsman's skill, Kipling forestalls any serious inquiry into his artistry. But his stories themselves often engage questions he refuses to address directly and can provide insights into his convictions and practices, his ideas about the nature of art, its toll on the artist, and its importance to society.

The term *artist* can be used both broadly and narrowly, however; it may refer to one who produces human works of beauty in any form or, more specifically, to one who produces visual aesthetic objects. In the broader sense, of course, the writer Kipling is an artist. But he also had a strong attraction to the visual, and this aspect of his work has received relatively scant attention: his long descriptions of visual details, his ability to create meaning through visual impressions, and his use of visual elements in metaphor and symbol.[24] Many critics emphasize the oral dimension of Kipling's work; certainly his reporter's ear for dialogue and the cool tone of many of his Anglo-Indian "turnovers" seem foreign to the delight in sensuous visible detail one usually associates with a painterly style. And, to be sure, dialogue is always important to Kipling. In his early tales he often seems to be sharpening his dialogic skills; "A Second-Rate Woman" is written almost entirely in dialogue; "The Hill of Illusion" and "Mrs Hauksbee Sits Out" are miniature plays, with no narrative voice. Even in as late a story as "The Wish House," the plot is carried almost entirely by the conversation between two women.

And yet, Kipling was, throughout his childhood and young adulthood, more surrounded by artists than writers. When Rudyard was born, his father, John Lockwood Kipling, was professor of architectural sculpture at the School of Art in Bombay. By the time Rudyard returned to India at the age of sixteen, his father was head of the School of Art in Lahore and curator of the Lahore Museum. John Lockwood Kipling illustrated many of his son's books. And, during his childhood years in England, Rudyard spent many winter holidays at the home of his aunt Georgiana and her husband, the Pre-Raphaelite painter Edward Burne-Jones.[25] Kipling later spoke lovingly of Burne-Jones, to whom he always felt close; at one point in his later life, Kipling and his family moved to Rottingdean, on the Sussex coast, to be near the Burne-Joneses.

Kipling himself was an inveterate sketcher, both in serious ways and as amusement. He illustrated his *Just So Stories*, and many of his manuscripts contain doodles, some exaggerated and comic, others delicate and evocative. Indeed, on the few occasions when Kipling directly discusses his work, he often uses visual images to describe his procedure. In *Something of Myself* he refers to the stories in *Rewards and Fairies* as made up of "three or four overlaid tints and textures, which might or might not reveal themselves according to the shifting light of sex, youth, and experience. It was like working lacquer and mother o'pearl" (111). He refers to his trouble in writing "The Eye of Allah" in terms of choosing the wrong visual model: "I had ridden off on hard black-and-white decoration, instead of pumicing the whole thing ivory-smooth, and loading it with thick colour and gilt" (122). Once his Daemon urges him to "treat it as an illuminated manuscript" (122), the work quickly assumes its satisfactory character.

Kipling's stories, from the earliest to the latest, reveal an instinct to use language for visual effect. One of his first tales, " 'The City of Dreadful Night' "(*LH*), provides an example of the way Kipling can pile up impressionistic details; describing a night walk into the city of Lahore, necessitated by a heat so intense that sleep was impossible, the narrator relates the sights he encountered. Kipling initiates his tale with a metaphor equating such heat and darkness with death. The suffocating air is depicted as a "dense wet heat that hung over the face of the land, like a blanket." The burial ground the narrator passes has had some of its bones dislodged and exposed by the heavy rains; he comments that "the heated air and the heavy earth has driven the very dead upward for coolness' sake." The bodies of men lying sleeping along the road become "like sheeted corpses." Even moonlight becomes a sepulchral glow, leper-like, suggestive of fear and death as surely as is the dark. The short piece is more a study than a story, an attempt at evoking a mood. Yet for all its metaphor and gothic effects, it focuses intently on the purely visible. Kipling may be working largely toward atmosphere, but he still gives his reader the look of the sleeping city, the quick glimpse of a woman's arm as she pulls a wandering child back to bed, emaciated dogs sniffing about the streets, the spectral stripes of moonlight on a mosque. "Doré might have drawn it," the narrator remarks, and it is clear that he is attempting to do the same. Kipling works with light and shadow, motion and stillness, and this plotless, characterless piece moves toward the stability of an artifact.

But this kind of description for its own sake, word painting one might call it, is not Kipling's typical procedure. Rather he tends to incorporate his landscape into an approach to character or theme. It is an understandable, though perhaps ironic, fact that the peripatetic Kipling's most developed visual images do indeed convey an acute sense of place. India provides him with a variety of loci, from the riding trails around Simla in "The Phantom 'Rickshaw" and "At the Pit's Mouth" through the panoramic geography of "William the Conqueror" to the dense Central Indian forest of the Jungle Books. Kipling's other major geographical focus is England, from the Puck books to "My Sunday at Home" (*DW*), "The House Surgeon," and " 'They.' " But he treats landscape and seascape in many other locales, from a Vermont farm in "A Walking Delegate" to a South African coastal prison in "The Captive" (*T&D*). His scenic descriptions, however, tend not to be gratuitous or merely for effect.

One curious example of Kipling's use of landscape is the imaginary world of George Cottar, "The Brushwood Boy." In the dream he began having when he was a child and continues into adulthood, Cottar progressively explores an imagined landscape, learning, as the years go by, the outlines and details of his visionary world: the Sea of Dreams, the downs and valleys, the deserts and islands. So familiar with his dreamscape does Cottar become that he maps it, filling in details as they accumulate and his knowledge increases. The particular dimensions of his imaginary world are not important; the existence of the landscape and its specific qualities becomes Cottar's link with Miriam, the young woman who has had the same dreams. What is remarkable, however, is Kipling's choice of an envisioned, particularized world as the form that Cottar's and Miriam's shared consciousness takes. Rather than dreaming of people, they dream of a place, instantly recognizable to both.

And Kipling makes it recognizable to the reader through long descriptions. Cottar's landscape evolves from a primitive scene such as a child might dream, a stack of brushwood, a beach, ships that can travel across dry land and sail into cardboard boxes, to an intricately developed, rich landscape, permanent enough to be drawn yet always retaining the slightly fantastic, disjointed quality that befits a dream, a world where objects can suddenly loom up and just as suddenly disappear from view. Through Cottar's dream life, Kipling is able to give the reader both a solid space and a hallucinatory experience.

Kipling attempted somewhat the same union of geography and disorientation in "The Bridge-Builders," published two years before "The Brushwood Boy." When Findlayson the engineer, overcome by opium and exhaustion, overhears a conversation among the beast gods of Hinduism, the richly vegetated divine landscape possesses the shimmering quality of a dream. Kipling, it is often noted, was infatuated with the minutiae of technology, but here he places that interest, embodied in the technological marvel of Findlayson's bridge, against the natural holiness of landscape, which becomes in this story, as it was for Cottar, the locus of a hidden spiritual life.

In "The Miracle of Purun Bhagat" (*SJB*), Kipling crystallizes the association between landscape and spirit. Purun Dass was as successful as it was possible for a native Indian to be under the Raj. Prime minister of one of the semiindependent native states, a friend of viceroys and governors, educated, cosmopolitan, powerful, honored, he abruptly resigns his position, puts aside his honors, and sets out barefoot, with a begging bowl, a wandering mendicant in search of peace. He travels north to the Himalayas, the land of his mother's people, and finally settles on a hillside within sight of a deserted shrine, overlooking a small village in the valley.

We travel with Purun Bhagat, as he is now known, Bhagat meaning "holy man." We survey the landscape panoramically and also move painstakingly through its hills and across its bridges. Kipling's technique is almost cinematic, beginning with a wide sweeping view, then focusing close enough to distinguish particular types of trees, and closing in on one spot.

> One evening he crossed the highest pass he had met till then—
> it had been a two days' climb—and came out on a line of snow-
> peaks that banded all the horizon—mountains from fifteen to
> twenty thousand feet high, looking almost near enough to hit
> with a stone, though they were fifty or sixty miles away.
> The pass was crowned with dense, dark forest—deodar, walnut,
> wild cherry, wild olive, and wild pear, but mostly deodar,
> which is the Himalayan cedar; and under the shadow of the
> deodars stood a deserted shrine to Kali.

The narrative perspective moves back and forth throughout the tale, from the vast to the particular, as we observe Purun Bhagat's communion with the immensity of nature and the simple routine of his days. In his mind, they are one, merely different ways of achieving the peace he desires.

Purun Bhagat's gentleness and stillness disarm the wild animals that frequent the shrine, and they come to consider him a friend. It is this solidarity that finally saves the lives of the villagers in the valley, for during a heavy rainy season, the hillside begins to break into an avalanche. The animals sense the impending danger and alert Purun Bhagat, who awakens the village and urges the inhabitants to flee. They are saved, but he is killed. The story ends with the villagers building a small shrine to the Bhagat.

The tale constructs a complex relationship between the meditative and the active life. Purun Bhagat renounces his successful career and all its worldly striving to become a seeker after peace. He moves slowly across the vast Indian landscape until he settles on his hillside, "the place appointed for him—the silence and the space." And there he stays as generations of life in the village pass. But he is shaken from his solitude by the floods and by his forgotten yet unextinguished sense of responsibility for other human beings. Purun Bhagat rushes to the village, shrieking in a voice unused for so long it sounds strange to his ears. The life of solitude must be relinquished when others' lives are endangered.

Kipling has associated in this story Purun Bhagat's spiritual life with the spacious, detailed landscape. But the Bhagat's choice, the safety of others, the necessity of action, mirrors the values so often upheld in Kipling's stories. The importance of human bonds and human action are praised. Here, passivity is given its greatest due; the Bhagat's pilgrimage to peace is lovingly described. But Kipling subordinates the visual splendor and the Bhagat's attachment to it to a different value.[26] Randall Jarrell has called this tale "tapestry-like,"[27] and the phrase captures its combination of scope and detail, the complexity of texture that yet contributes to a large view. But the story also suggests Kipling's growing inclination to develop the visual, associate it with a good, yet place it within a larger morality.

In "Kaa's Hunting," the audacious Monkey-People, the Banderlog, abduct Mowgli and carry him to Cold Lairs, a ruined Indian city. Kipling devotes a number of long descriptive passages to this eerily beautiful site. The first portrays it from the vantage point of the decaying palace that overlooks it. "From the palace you could see the rows and rows of roofless houses that made up the city looking like empty honeycombs filled with blackness." Kipling's vivid description continues as we move toward one particular spot, an old, broken terrace where the Bander-log deposit Mowgli.

> There was a ruined summer-house of white marble in the center of the terrace, built for queens dead a hundred years ago. The domed roof had half fallen in and blocked up the underground passage from the palace by which the queens used to enter; but the walls were made of screens of marble tracery—beautiful milk-white fretwork, set with agates and cornelians and jasper and lapis lazuli, and as the moon came up behind the hill it shone through the open-work, casting shadows on the ground like black velvet embroidery.

By setting this evocative description, which conveys the emptiness, decay, and dignity of the ruin, within a larger section filled with the sudden, ineffectual movement and noise of the monkeys, Kipling intensifies the silence and beauty of the scene. The passage is filled with color, white, black, red, green, and blue. And the colors are allied to textures, cool marble, hard jewels, and the intricate tracery of embroidery. It is a scene one could easily imagine being painted.

But Kipling uses resources of language unavailable to the painter. By combining the long "a" assonances and smooth sibilants of "agates," "jasper," "lapis lazuli," with the linking "and," he slows down the reader's progress, making him or her pause momentarily at each of these words; they are linked, yet the use of "and" makes each distinct. Juxtaposing the compound words "milk-white fretwork," with their hard consonants and short vowels, conveys the abrupt, broken effect of the tracery. Against the visible, tactile immediacy of this scene, Kipling then conjures the ghosts of the queens who are no more. These figures, who do not exist literally but are a powerful presence, a beautiful testimony to mortality, give a human poignancy to what had been a mere physical site. While appealing to the reader's vision, Kipling yet gives his passage what painting cannot; the sounds of the words contribute to the reader's sense of texture, and the visible dimension of the passage becomes part of a larger emotional resonance than mere mimesis could provide.

The permanence of the English landscape is a major underlying assumption on which the Puck books, *Puck of Pook's Hill* and *Rewards and Fairies*, are built. Kipling devotes considerable space to evoking the richness and specificity of Dan and Una's haunts, but his purpose is not just to convey the precise impression of the English landscape; it is to suggest its permanence, mark its similarity to the land in earlier times. Many of the tales open with an exact description of trees or flowers or brooks. In "Young Men at the Manor," he describes a fishing spot. "In the pools you could see the wave thrown up by the trouts as they charged hither and yon, and the pools were joined to each other—except in flood time, when all was one brown rush—by sheets of thin broken water that poured themselves chuckling round the darkness of the next bend." The verbs "thrown up," "charged," "poured" are complemented by nouns and adjectives that imply motion as well, "flood time," "brown rush," "sheets of broken water." Even "chuckling," which should suggest sound, seems by its association with the movement and direction of the water to stress activity; it becomes more a visible than an aural aspect of the water.

Dan and Una are getting ready to leave their seaside vacation home in "Brother Square-Toes" (*R&F*), and Kipling pauses to describe the look of the sea. "The tide was dead low under the chalk cliffs, and the little wrinkled waves grieved along the sands up the coast to Newhaven and down the coast to long, grey Brighton, whose smoke trailed out across the Channel." Combining the impression of a vista, its emphasis on the lengthy coast and the trail of smoke, with the close and textured motion of "wrinkled waves," Kipling again moves quickly between panorama and precise observation, the shift in focus so familiar in his visual descriptions. And the vividness of "wrinkled" to describe the waves' appearance reminds us that Kipling is not only a writer of fiction but also a poet.

" 'They' " contains some of Kipling's most notable descriptions of landscape, here during different seasons and different times of day. The tale's use of intricate visual effect extends to the interior of the manor house as well. And Miss Florence, blind from infancy, reveals that she sees the moods of people as colors, harsh and brilliant or subdued and gentle. Ultimately, however, the painterly quality of this story is revealed to be inadequate, as literal sight, despite the rich pleasures it brings, is shown to be less desirable than spiritual sight, insight. In what may be his most intense use of color, light, and shadow, Kipling takes his estimate of the pleasures such effects can and cannot give.

The narrator's three excursions to the manor house take place at different times of the year, late spring, summer, and autumn. He describes the landscape in meticulous detail, its "liquid sunshine," "moss-cankered oak and beech"; he speaks of a ground where "primrose-clumps showed like jade, and a few sickly, white-stalked bluebells nodded together." The house is surrounded by an intricately trimmed hedge, made to look like horsemen and ladies and fantastic animals. At last, the house itself appears, "an ancient house of lichened and weatherworn stone, with mullioned windows and roofs of red-rose tile." Shape and color and texture are all central to the narrator's description. Kipling gives extensive space to the narrator's view of his last, autumnal visit. We see the late flowers, the beginning signs of decaying leaves, the thickened air. And the narrator gives particular attention to the look of the Channel as he rides in sight of its edges. "As I reached the crest of the Downs I felt the soft air change, saw it glaze under the sun; and, looking down at the sea, in that instant beheld the blue of the Channel turn, through polished silver and dulled steel, to dingy pewter."

Almost Pre-Raphaelite in his attempt to capture the look of light in nature, its changing hue as weather or seasons or time of day change, Kipling can extend the same care to the description of interior space. "The red light poured itself along the age-polished dusky panels till the Tudor roses and lions of the gallery took colour and motion." Much that is memorable in this story can be attributed to the setting. Conversations take place in particularly realized contexts, and meaning becomes heavily intertwined with color. But Miss Florence's gift, though she is blind, is a certain kind of sight—she "could see the naked soul." And the narrator must learn to see the truth of his own loss, his daughter's death, accept it fully, and put it in its place as he returns to the world. As the narrator makes a physical progress to the house, at first allowed only into the garden but, as he proves his kindness, accepted into the home of the children, he makes a spiritual journey into his own heart. He first speaks of, then touches, his daughter, recognizes fully his loss, and recognizes too that he must never return to this house. He will move out from the center of the house to the periphery, the garden, and to the world outside. Kipling organizes the space of the story to give us both the intensely detailed view and the panorama, the move from a distant glimpse to knowledge and then the willingness to draw away again.

In many of his stories, then, Kipling devotes considerable space to a delicate visual scene. He pauses to give his reader the exact nuance of color, of light and shadow, of movement or stillness. And he is masterful in marshalling the resources of language to create his effects, intensifying visible and tactile impressions by the quality of his descriptions. In his very control of language to achieve an effect beyond that which the visible can provide, Kipling demonstrates the ways in which, in his work, word painting is not sufficient. He does more than supplement the vividness of his scenes with nonvisual devices; he often subordinates their beauty to a thematic effect. Beauty becomes broken, lost, or forsaken because other values must be chosen.

Kipling's use of space often becomes symbolic; his treatments of distance and perspective, his juxtaposition of inner and outer, often function as an exploration of sacred and profane space. He frequently sees interior space as a sanctuary from the world, as he does in " 'They' "; Ameera's house in "Without Benefit of Clergy" is another pro-minent example; so too is Amir Nath's Gully in "Beyond the

Pale." But this latter tale introduces an ironic reversal Kipling sometimes employs; the sanctuary can become the trap or the prison as Kashima does, surrounded by the Dosehri Hills in "A Wayside Comedy." Kipling's visual imagination makes itself apparent in a wide variety of ways, in description, in theme, and in symbol.

In his first novel, *The Light that Failed*, distinctly autobiographical though heavily disguised in its incidents, Kipling creates an artist as hero, one whose genius is in depicting realistic, often violent adventure. And Kipling has a handful of stories that treat the artist's experience as the concentration of the aesthetic.[28] In "The Eye of Allah" (*D&C*), John of Burgos, a medieval illuminator, astonishes those who see his work with his realism; his devils embody no abstract idea of evil; they suggest, in their specificity and vitality, an art based on observation. John claims he draws what he sees, and like Browning's Fra Lippo Lippi, his fidelity to fact, independent of canonical preferences, shocks his audience.[29]

But Kipling does not so much use the painter as his hero in dealing with art as he uses images or metaphors from visual art when writing of aesthetic experience. In "Wressley of the Foreign Office" (*PTH*), the central character is a middle-aged civil servant in India. Famous for his expertise in intricate Indian politics, Wressley, in order to impress a young woman, begins to write a history, *Native Rule in Central India*. With vast knowledge and prodigious discipline, he writes his magnum opus, only to be laughed at by the frivolous, uncomprehending girl. Kipling's tale is slight, but deals in a few pages with questions of art, work, and love. And, though it is a book Wressley is writing, Kipling weaves his descriptions of Wressley's efforts with language drawn from the world of visual art. He introduces Wressley in his Indian setting. "One of the many curses of our life in India is the want of atmosphere in the painter's sense. There are no half-tints worth noticing. Men should stand out all crude and raw, with nothing to tone them down, and nothing to scale them against." Wressley is a "frigid workman"; "he needed the white light of local colour on his palette."

Kipling deals with larger questions of the artist and art in a number of stories, some evoking the visual sense, but others relying on a more complex sensuous description. He treats the writer's work synesthetically in " 'Wireless' " (*T&D*), a story built on the conceit of defining poetic inspiration as akin to electrical induction. Set during the early days of wireless transmission, the tale recounts the experience of three young men: an amateur transmitter, waiting for a signal from

Poole; the narrator, an acquaintance who has a dilettante's interest in the new technology; and an assistant chemist in the shop where the story takes place. Shaynor, the young chemist, ill from tuberculosis, sips an alcoholic drink concocted by the narrator and, in a semi-drugged state, begins to draft passages from Keats's "Eve of St. Agnes" and "Ode to a Nightingale." As the narrator watches breathlessly, Shaynor writes and rewrites his lines, slowly coming closer to Keats's. Before he fully succeeds, he emerges from his stupor, unaware of what he has done. The tale concludes with the three men going back to their normal lives.

The theory of poetic inspiration that underlies the story is a fantastic variation on Kipling's own belief that the artist receives his power from a force larger than he.[30] The tale defines the force as akin to electricity. Kipling's narrator can make no sense of what he has witnessed, and does not try to. And the reader too is left with the puzzle unsolved.

The narrator theorizes that the confluence of circumstances in Shaynor's life makes him susceptible to the Keatsian inspiration: his tuberculosis; his work as a chemist; his love for the lower-class, vivacious Fanny Brand. And Kipling creates an atmosphere that evokes the "Eve of St. Agnes," an enclosed space of light and color, protected from a biting cold and howling wind.

> The dried pavement seemed to rough up in goose-flesh under the scouring of the savage wind, and we could hear, long ere he passed, the policeman flapping his arms to keep himself warm. Within, the flavours of cardamoms and chloric-ether disputed those of the pastilles and a score of drugs and perfume and soap scents. Our electric lights, set low down in the windows before the tun-bellied Rosamund jars, flung inward three monstrous daubs of red, blue, and green, that broke into kaleidoscopic lights on the faceted knobs of the drug-drawers, the cut-glass scent flagons, and the bulbs of the sparklet bottles. They flushed the white-tiled floor in gorgeous patches; splashed along the nickel-silver counter rails, and turned the polished mahogany counter-panels to the likeness of intricate grained marbles— slabs of porphyry and malachite.

The ambiance of the mundane chemist's shop is transformed into a brilliant Keatsian array of sweet and pungent scents, colored lights reflected in faceted glass, textures of grained wood and cool marble. By surrounding the poor and dying Shaynor with an intense sensuousness, Kipling captures the Keatsian contrast between bright beauty and mortality. The power of Shaynor's gift, of which he is unaware, is captured in Kipling's descriptions; the poetry of the story is not in Shaynor's language as it approximates Keats's, but in Kipling's.

The artist figures prominently in a late story, "The Bull that Thought" (*D&C*). Kipling invests this tale of an extraordinary bull, one able to tease and defeat any human antagonist, with a frame and with numerous allusions, similes, and metaphors to make clear Apis the bull represents human aesthetic creativity. The bull, powerful, amoral, and keenly aware of his superiority to all he encounters, whether they be other animals or human beings, is a most dangerous force on the small farm. He is finally sent to the bull ring in a provincial Spanish town.

Formerly Apis had demonstrated his intelligence and power by killing rival bulls. Now he has the opportunity to perform in an appropriate arena, before a large audience. He quickly dispatches the various picadors and capeadors sent out to test him, and does so in a cunning fashion, as if his tossing and goring were an accident. He is saving his true skill for the right antagonist. Voiron, who witnesses the scene, realizes Apis's seeming casualness is only a mask to lure a worthy matador, to attract a worthy opponent. "Then, Monsieur, I began to comprehend that it was an artist we had to deal with." Having either killed or frightened away all others, Apis confronts the aging Chisto, himself a product of the farm, comfortable with bulls. Together, each taking the other's measure and acknowledging a respect, they perform a kind of dance.

> Apis trusted himself as Chisto trusted him, and, this time, he conformed to the man, with inimitable judgment and temper. He allowed himself to be played into the shadow or the sun, as the delighted audience demanded. He raged enormously; he feigned defeat; he despaired in statuesque abandon, and thence flashed into fresh paroxysms of wrath but always with the detachment of the true artist who knows he is but the vessel of an emotion whence others, not he, must drink.

Apis's intellect and energy allow him to destroy anything that comes in his way. And he revels in that power. But destruction does not reveal his true talent. When presented with the proper arena, antagonist, and circumstance, he harnesses his energy, demonstrates restraint and an awareness of others; it is in self-imposed limitation that he best expresses his potential, a dance of power, danger, comedy, and grace. The artist needs constraint and pressure to channel his power toward aesthetic form. Apis, for all his intelligence, can perform at his peak only when he is confronted with the challenge of a second-rate matador who yet respects and understands him, a sympathetic soul who willingly acts to allow Apis his glory. And Apis returns the gift; he cavorts with Chisto, making the old man feel young again.

The tale, which recounts the need for control to achieve the highest level of accomplishment, is itself a model of aesthetic complexity. With a double frame—an unnamed English narrator stopping at a French country inn, being told the story of Apis by Voiron, the second narrator, who had witnessed Apis's triumph—the story provides a variety of examples of great power brought under control. As the story opens, the Englishman is preparing to test his motorcar for speed. The right night, weather, moonlight, and road all coincide propitiously. The car's speed is record breaking. Voiron, who had asked to be present at the test, is so delighted he invites the Englishman to share a bottle of wine; the wine, it is revealed, is a legendary champagne of the district, so rare it is cultivated for the growers only, an exceptionally refined product of nature, nature controlled by art, just as the motor car suggests enormous power controlled by the intelligence and skill of the driver.

"The Bull that Thought" presents art as a harnessing of a power almost demonic; by creating a bull to represent the artist, Kipling implies that the artistic impulse is irrational, amoral, brutal, even lethal.[31] The artist's reward is the awareness of his performance; he will give pleasure to his audience, but he retains an element of detachment. It is himself he ultimately pleases. As a bull, Apis is permanently isolated from his audience, supercilious and disdainful of the mere humans who cheer him.

The relationship between the artist and his audience is explored differently in Kipling's mythic tale, "The Children of the Zodiac" (*MI*). Leo and the Girl, Virgo, are two of the six Children of the Zodiac; all other zodiacal characters belong to the Six Houses, a dangerous collection. The Children begin as immortal, but, by choosing to submit themselves to human will, to labor and to suffer, they come to share human mortality.

Leo and the Girl confront their fate through love and art. Deciding never to leave each other and instead to laugh at their enemy, they move fully into the world of men and women, and Leo begins to sing, but people crowd round and plead for more and still more, and Leo finds he must sing in weariness and pain as well as in pleasure. He comes to detest his new life; he is exhausted, impecunious, homeless. And his listeners do not appreciate his effort. He is helpful and, finally, necessary to them, but never understood. But he and the Girl continue. And his songs have only one refrain, "that whatever came or did not come the children of men must not be afraid." Finally he knows that he is about to die. Fearful at first, he finally accepts his death, having learned the lesson he himself taught.

Simple in narrative and language, the story presents a straightforward view of the artist's role. At first Leo sings to confront his own fear, but, learning of his power to comfort others, he takes that burden on himself. At once an integral part of others' confrontation with their own mortality and yet forever separated from them by his lineage and gift, he lives on the threshold of human community, valued but set apart. But his song is as necessary to his own comfort as it is to others'.

Leo's artistic gift is not seen as something violent or dangerous, as Apis's was. But the power that charms and wins audiences also isolates the artist. Like a god or a demon, he lives aware of his uniqueness, his gift and his mission.

The story focuses on questions of art, mortality, and community, but expresses many familiar Kipling themes. Leo and the Girl watch as human beings struggle to live when all is taken from them, a situation that pervades many of Kipling's late stories. Equally central to Kipling's concerns is the emphasis on work. The Children of the Zodiac find their lives' meaning in human work; it provides community and prevents them from thinking of the death they know awaits them. But it is art that makes work bearable. Artists can for a moment forget the dreariness of life and help others to forget. But the reality of death returns; art cannot affect that, but it can shape the attitude with which men and women approach it. Art, in this story, subsumes the role of religion. It becomes the highest expression of the human spirit.

The story is testimony to Kipling's high regard for his work, though he rarely writes directly about his artistry. In the course of a long career he saw his reputation soar and plummet. It is perhaps now, with the distance of years and our growing understanding of the complexities of the

colonial and postcolonial worlds, that readers can approach Kipling
with fewer assumptions. His work begins to seem both more accessible and more demanding. His short stories, from the first to the last,
reveal a core of persistent concerns. Perhaps the most pervasive is his
understanding of isolation and loneliness. From the earliest Anglo-
Indian tales of men and women, both shallow and seasoned, finding
the geographical remoteness and cultural deracination of the Empire
to be overpowering, to the very last tales of parents adrift because
their beloved children have died, Kipling locates a deep human fear.
The story he spins around it changes as he grows older and experiences the various forms that fear may take. Existential loneliness, we
may term it now, or the quest for integration, but Kipling knew and
described the feeling well.

John Bayley remarks that Kipling is out of fashion today because he
emphasizes "the disciplines of the pack" rather than "the gratuitous
act of the solitary and alienated consciousness."[32] But Kipling's emphasis on the pack, the social unit, derives in large part from his understanding of isolation. He is drawn to the comradeship, cohesion,
and order society brings because he is so acutely aware of the psychological terror and moral vacuity isolation can bring. Because he is
drawn to those characters who struggle against incoherence and despair, he may at first seem a writer less suited to twentieth-century
tastes, more in the Victorian mainstream than those who chronicle
more insistently a state of alienation. But there can be no doubt, when
one reads widely among his stories, that Kipling could create a portrait
of the solitary mind.

In very many of his stories, though, Kipling dwells on those strategies and ruses human beings employ to deal with their isolation. He is
the celebrant of work as a gesture of solidarity and a cry of defiance
against despair. His stories of work, in trade, in Empire, in war, rein-
scribe some of his deepest values: loyalty, fidelity, perseverance,
knowledge. It is in these terms one can best understand Kipling's attitude toward the Empire as an arena for humanity's best work, a place
where daily labor can be put to the common good. Kipling's imperialism is still for many readers the sticking point, the obstacle to their enjoyment. And no one can deny the racism announced in many of the
Anglo-Indian tales. And yet, a close reading of at least some of those
tales reveals a narrative frame that undermines the characters and
their complacency, making Kipling's point of view harder to determine. Kipling's Anglo-Indian stories often suggest a complex artistry

as well as the sense that they were written by a man who had seen enough of India to believe there were no villains and few heroes among those he encountered. Kipling was capable of a subtle, sensitive portrayal of the consequences of imperialism on the oppressed. He does not see the Indians under the Raj in the kinds of terms we might perceive them today. He does not treat Indians as robbed of their land, their independence, their culture. Rather, he describes the tragic consequences that can ensue when two peoples, in the closest proximity, are yet the products of profoundly different cultures. Kipling is pessimistic about the ability of individuals to transcend such barriers, and in the few stories in which he treats their attempts to do so, characters end in suffering or death. Whether true friendship or love can succeed between the Indians and English is a question that pervades the colonial novel, from Kipling to E. M. Forster.[33] Kipling repeatedly suggests it cannot.

Love, successful and often unsuccessful, remains one of the great mysteries in Kipling's stories. He writes of love so powerful it can save another, can give meaning to life even when one is approaching death, can outlast death and continue to sustain those who live on. Kipling has many stories of brutality, revenge, violence, and anger, stories that reveal a meanness of spirit that alienates some readers. But, finally, even his hoaxes can turn protective. In "Dayspring Mishandled" (*L&R*), Manallace, who has spent years concocting a humiliating retribution for his enemy, Castorley, finally takes pity on his victim as Castorley lies dying, and decides to devote himself to protecting Castorley's reputation. The story finally demonstrates the hollowness of revenge: it absorbs the energy of the revenger but destroys him in the process. Manallace extricates himself from this seemingly ineluctable descent and saves himself by commitment to Castorley's honor.

"Dayspring Mishandled," while inverting the usual progress of Kipling's hoax stories, typifies the increasingly complex use of narrative frames one finds in Kipling's work. The early Anglo-Indian tales regularly provide a narrator who is close enough to the situation to understand it but distanced enough to judge it wryly. The "three musketeer" stories of Mulvaney, Learoyd, and Ortheris often employ two narrators, the soldier who witnessed the event and speaks of it in heavy dialect through a military perspective, and the civilian layman who interprets and comments on the action and characters. Many of the Anglo-Indian tales begin from the assumption that the truth of the situation can never be known. Cultural barriers are too great and one cannot know the mind of the Other, or the clash of cultures creates confusion and no single truth can emerge. In "His Chance in Life" the narrator describes the borderline people, those with a mix of black and white blood. Only they understand each other, and it will take a borderline poet to explain them to us. "In the meantime, any stories about them cannot be absolutely correct in fact or inference." Even gender can be delimiting. A man cannot fully understand the mind of a woman. Therefore, in "False Dawn" (*PTH*), the narrator admits, before he begins, that the story needs a woman to tell it. Lacking that, "the tale must be told from the outside—in the dark—all wrong." Kipling's early stories often give the impression of a sharp, quick view of a situation that is yet undercut by the narrator's confessed ignorance about its meaning.

As his work progresses, Kipling's narrative strategies become more complex. "Mrs Bathurst" is notoriously ambiguous, but "The Man Who Would Be King," though at first straightforward in its multiple narration, seduces the reader into identifying with a seemingly objective speaker who then implicates himself in a dubious venture. Similarly, in "Dayspring Mishandled" the narrative "I," at first a bystander to the action, becomes almost an accomplice with Manallace, at least a knowing, willing companion. The reader has his sympathies bounced between the insulted Manallace and the dying Castorley as the narrator himself shifts uneasily between the two. And Kipling can produce a narrative voice that seems so artlessly close to an experience, as in " 'They,' " that the reader seems to participate in the action, learning as the narrator learns, sympathizing fully with him in his pain.

J. M. S. Tompkins compares Kipling's last stories with novellas; the whole life of the protagonist is sketched in, not as background, but as integral to the episode that the reader observes, that episode becoming the distillation of a life in a moment.[34] C. A. Bodelson agrees, arguing the late Kipling works not in the mode of the modern short story, impressionism, but in the form of a highly concentrated novel, with several layers of meaning, symbolic effects, and a text that develops through repetition of language and images as well as through cross-references within the work. These may be effects we associate with longer fiction, but Bodelson suggests another parallel; Kipling was trying to create, he argues, a short story that had the effect of poetry.[35]

Whether in or out of academic fashion, Kipling has always had a large popular readership. There is a contingent, to be sure, who cannot warm to these tales. They find Kipling's emotions too unshaded, his attitude too cynical, his style too declamatory; they believe he lacks a real analysis of character; they find his human sympathies vulgar and his political sympathies authoritarian. But there still remains a legion of Kipling readers. His sure narrative drive, vivid characters, realistic dialogue, all evident from the earliest stories, have drawn many. Some, reared on the children's stories, are devoted to the Jungle Books and the Puck books. And others value the more ruminative postwar tales, with their sense of a joy irretrievably lost. In recent years, a number of scholars have explored the artistry of the tales, have argued for an emotional and aesthetic complexity not hitherto generally accorded Kipling. Indeed, when one examines the extraordinary variety of these tales, their artistic economy, breadth of sympathy, intuitive understanding of moral crisis, one knows one is confronting a brilliant writer. Kipling will never again achieve the virtually universal approval he enjoyed early in his career, but his work can be appreciated anew by those interested in the short story as practiced by a virtuoso.

Notes to Part I

1. *Life's Handicap* (*LH*). Because there are so many editions of Kipling's works readily available, library sets, inexpensive sets, anthologies, paperbacks, it seems to be most helpful not to refer to the pagination of a particular edition, but to the short-story collection in which the particular story under discussion first appeared and in which it is still most often reprinted. The references to these collections will appear, as abbreviations, within the text after the first reference to the story. For a complete list of abbreviations, see the Selected Bibliography, Collections of Short Stories. As my own source, I have used *The Collected Works of Rudyard Kipling* (New York: AMS Press, 1970), a reprint of the *Burwash Edition* (New York: Doubleday, Doran and Company Inc., 1941), itself following *The Sussex Edition* (London: Macmillan, 1937–39); Kipling was working on this last edition at the time of his death.

2. J. M. S. Tompkins, *The Art of Rudyard Kipling* (Lincoln: University of Nebraska Press, 1959), 185; hereafter cited in the text. Tompkins devotes a chapter to "Man and the Abyss."

3. Nora Crook, *Kipling's Myths of Love and Death* (Basingstoke: Macmillan, 1989), 96ff.; hereafter cited in the text.

4. See Hugh Haughton's introduction to *Wee Willie Winkie* (London: Penguin, 1988), 34–37, for a discussion of the political implications of the tale.

5. See, for example, C. E. Carrington, " 'Baa, Baa, Black Sheep': Fact or Fiction," *Kipling Journal* 39 (June 1972): 714. Angus Wilson also discusses the relationship between the events at Southsea and Kipling's treatment of them in *The Strange Ride of Rudyard Kipling: His Life and Works* (London: Secker & Warburg, 1977), 17–34.

6. Alice Macdonald Fleming, "My Brother, Rudyard Kipling (1)," in *Kipling: Interviews and Recollections*, ed. Harold Orel (Totowa, N.J.: Barnes and Noble Books, 1983), 1, 9.

7. Bonamy Dobrée, in *The Lamp and the Lute*, suggests this attitude succinctly. "With the introspective movement which found its prophet in Rousseau, with the hysterical subjective idealists whose only reality is their emotion, he will have nothing to do, and it is likely that Proust seems a dreary waste to him." In *Kipling and the Critics*, ed. Elliot L. Gilbert (New York: New York University Press, 1965), 50.

8. For a full discussion of Carlyle's influence on Kipling, see Crook, 33–40.

9. There have been numerous attacks on Kipling's politics, often mixed with a criticism of his aggressive temperament. The most virulent early response to Kipling was Robert Buchanan's *The Voice of the Hooligan: A Discussion of Kiplingism*, published in 1900. Buchanan dismisses Kipling's verse as repre-

sentative of the tone of the age's journalism, "its vulgarity, its flippancy, and its radical unintelligence" (26–27). He writes of Kipling, "he represents, with more or less accuracy, what the mob is thinking, and for this very reason he is likely to be forgotten as swiftly and summarily as he has been applauded" (27). "He has scarely on any single occasion uttered anything that does not suggest moral baseness, or hover dangerously near it" (27). Of *Stalky & Co.*, Buchanan writes, "the vulgarity, the brutality, the savagery, reeks on every page. . . . And the moral of the book—for, of course, like all such banalities, it professes to have a moral—is that out of materials like these is fashioned the humanity which is to ennoble and preserve our Anglo-Saxon empire" (31). But later, more temperate readers of strong political convictions who appreciate Kipling's talent still find themselves forced to admit their distaste for his ideas, which, again, they find a function of his temperament. Two of the most notable are George Orwell and Lionel Trilling. In an essay in *Dickens, Dali, and Others*, published in 1946, Orwell begins a judicious and subtle estimate of Kipling's work by proclaiming, "there is a definite strain of sadism in him, over and above the brutality which a writer of that type has to have. Kipling *is* a jingo imperialist, he *is* morally insensitive and aesthetically disgusting. It is better to start by admitting that, and then try to find out why it is that he survives while the refined people who have sniggered at him seem to wear so badly" (74–75). And, in 1949, in *The Liberal Imagination*, Trilling writes of T. S. Eliot's remark that Kipling was a tory not a fascist. Trilling responds, "a tory, to be sure, is not a fascist, and Kipling is not properly called a fascist. . . . His toryism often had in it a lower-middle-class snarl of defeated gentility, and it is this, rather than his love of authority and force, that might suggest an affinity with facism [*sic*]. His imperialism is reprehensible not because it *is* imperialism but because it is a puny and mindless imperialism" (95). The above essays are all reprinted in Elliot L. Gilbert, ed. *Kipling and the Critics* (New York: New York University Press, 1965). Page references are to this edition.

10. See Elliot Gilbert's chapter by that title ("Imperialism as Metaphor") in *The Good Kipling*.

11. Shamsul Islam, *Kipling's "Law": A Study of his Philosophy of Life* (New York: St. Martin's Press, 1975), 83.

12. The story has accumulated a considerable body of criticism and provides a good example of the spectrum of approaches to Kipling's work. It is treated in virtually every full-length study as well as in numerous periodical essays. For a reading that focuses on the effect of the narrative frame, for example, see Tim Bascom, "Secret Imperialism: The Reader's Response to the Narrator in 'The Man Who Would Be King'," *English Literature in Transition, 1880–1920* 31 (1988): 162–73. Jeffrey Meyers, on the other hand, stresses the tale's straightforward exploration of imperialism; see "The Idea of Moral Authority in 'The Man Who Would Be King'," *Studies in English Literature* 8 (1968): 711–23.

13. Bonamy Dobrée, *Rudyard Kipling: Realist and Fabulist* (London: Oxford University Press, 1967). See Dobrée's section, "The Fabulist," 145–67.

14. See, for example, Ann Parry, " 'Take away that bauble!' Political Allegory in 'Below the Mill Dam,' " *Kipling Journal* 62 (December 1988): 10–21.

15. J. I. M. Stewart, *Rudyard Kipling* (New York: Dodd, Mead & Company, 1966), 138; hereafter cited in the text.

16. The distribution of stories between *The Jungle Book* and *The Second Jungle Book* varies from edition to edition. In discussing a short story, I have referred to Kipling's original arrangement (as presented in the Selected Bibliography). Many modern editions follow this arrangement as well. But, in the 1897 "Outward Bound" edition of Kipling's work, the stories were reordered. *The Jungle Book* contained the Mowgli stories; *The Second Jungle Book* contained the non-Mowgli tales. This arrangement was maintained in the Sussex edition and in the AMS edition I have followed in all other respects throughout this study.

17. Unlike many critics, John McBratney, in "Imperial Subjects, Imperial Space in Kipling's *Jungle Book*," *Victorian Studies* 35 (1992): 277–93, argues that "In the Rukh" is important to understanding the Mowgli stories. McBratney's larger focus is on nineteenth-century ethnographic theories and their relationship to the Jungle Books.

18. See Daniel Karlin's introduction to *The Jungle Book* (London, Penguin Books, 1987), 23–24.

19. In *Something of Myself*, Kipling discusses the way in which this line supports the volume. "My doubt cleared itself with the first tale 'Cold Iron,' which gave me my underwood: 'What else could I have done?'—the plinth of all structures" (111).

20. Angus Wilson, in *The Strange Ride of Rudyard Kipling*, 292–93, examines, from a different perspective the cyclical view of history found in the Puck books. The late nineteenth century was haunted by a sense of decline, from the loss of faith in orthodox Christianity to the incipient erosion of the Empire. A faith in historical cycles, popular at this time, argues Wilson, provided a comfort to many thoughtful people, gave them a hope that the period of decay was only a necessary prelude to an intellectual and political rebirth.

21. This preface appears in only a few editions of Kipling's stories. See *The Phantom 'Rickshaw and Other Tales* (London: Sampson Low, Marston, Searle, & Rivington, Ld., n.d.), 3.

22. A brief list of critical treatments might include John Bayley, *The Uses of Division: Unity and Disharmony in Literature* (London: Chatto and Windus, 1976); C. A. Bodelson, *Aspects of Kipling's Art* (Manchester: Manchester University Press, 1964); Elliot L. Gilbert, *The Good Kipling;* Philip Mason, *Kipling: The Glass, the Shadow, and the Fire* (New York: Harper & Row, 1975); Philip Mason, "Two Kipling Puzzles," *Kipling Journal* (September 1988): 25–34; T.

C. W. Stinton, "What Really Happened in 'Mrs Bathurst'?" *Essays in Criticism* 38 (1988): 55–74; Ruth Waterhouse, " 'That Blindish Look': Significance of Meaning in 'Mrs Bathurst,' " *Studia Neophilologica* 60, no. 2 (1988): 193–206.

23. See, for example, Kipling's lectures on "Fiction" and "Literature," reprinted in the next part of this volume, "The Writer."

24. Two critics in particular do devote considerable attention to the visual elements in Kipling's short stories: Nora Crook, in *Kipling's Myths of Love and Death*, and A. G. Sandison, in "Rudyard Kipling," *British Writers*, ed. Ian Scott-Kilvert, vol. 6 (New York: Charles Scribner's Sons, 1983).

25. A. G. Sandison argues that Kipling's attitudes toward English history and the integral relationship between art and daily work bear strong resemblances to the beliefs of William Morris, an occasional visitor to the Burne-Jones home during the times Kipling stayed there.

26. "The Miracle of Purun Bhagat," of course, explores in miniature some major concerns in Kipling's greatest novel, *Kim*. The Bhagat embodies within himself the competing impulses toward withdrawal and activity that are separated into the characters of the lama and Kim.

27. Randall Jarrell, "In the Vernacular," in *Kipling, Auden & Co.: Essays and Reviews, 1935–1964* (New York: Farrar, Strauss and Giroux, 1980), 355.

28. For a general survey of Kipling's depictions of the artist, see David H. Stewart, "Kipling's Portraits of the Artist," *English Literature in Transition, 1880–1920* 31 (1988): 265–83.

29. Fra Lippo Lippi, though not mentioned directly in this story, is a figure Kipling often refers to. In *Something of Myself*, he calls the early Renaissance painter "a not too remote—I dare to think—ancestor of mine" (22).

30. In *Kipling's Hidden Narratives* (Oxford: Basil Blackwell, 1988), Sandra Kemp emphasizes the visual aspect of the theory of inspiration adumbrated in the story. The tale distinguishes between Keats the poet and Keats as a metonym for the language of his poetry. "Writing is more than writing. The 'blindfold soul' which Keats and Mr Shaynor share within the wheel of life exists in the unconscious and in language. Indeed, writing becomes a metaphor for preternatural seeing" (36).

31. Elliot L. Gilbert discusses the violence and brutality inherent in Kipling's view of art as implied by "The Bull that Thought" in *The Good Kipling*, 168–87.

32. Bayley, *The Uses of Division*, 65.

33. This subject is a major concern of Jeffrey Meyers in *Fiction and the Colonial Experience* (Ipswich, N.H.: Boydell Press, 1973).

34. Tompkins details the ways in which the last stories achieve condensed complexity. She concludes that "Kipling came to master the material of the novel, but he did it by relinquishing the novel form" (7).

35. See chapter 6, "Kipling's Late Manner," in *Aspects of Kipling's Art* (Manchester: Manchester University Press, 1964).

Part 2

THE WRITER

Introduction

Kipling was always reluctant to speak directly about himself or his work. He avoided those critics who took, he thought, a prying interest in his life; their efforts he called a "higher cannibalism." He was proud, instead, to let his fiction and verse speak for themselves, without explanation or apology.

Two of his public addresses, on "Literature" and "Fiction," suggest his reasons. The writer has a great gift, but not one he has chosen or can entirely control. He does not experience great events but has the miraculous power of finding the language to re-create them in the reader's mind. Indeed, he creates the truth of events; there is no truth, Kipling believes, until the artist provides it. Characteristically, however, Kipling expresses his mimetic, vatic theory of art elliptically, through stories rather than through analysis.

Kipling is somewhat more direct in his autobiography, *Something of Myself*, though, here too, he leans toward metaphor. In his remarks about his "Daemon," he reiterates his view of the artist as the voice of a power not his own. But in his brief descriptions of his writing habits, his walks during which he would collect ideas and impressions, his penchant for revision and severe editing, we catch a glimpse of the craftsman at work. And here he mentions a favorite artistic figure, Browning's Fra Lippo Lippi, whose realism, energy, and courage Kipling warmed to as a model of what the artist should be.

"Literature"

A great, and I frankly admit, a somewhat terrifying, honour has come to me; but I think, compliments apart, that the most case-hardened worker in letters, speaking to such an assembly as this, must recognise the gulf that separates even the least of those who do things worthy to be written about from even the best of those who have written things worthy of being talked about.

There is an ancient legend which tells us that when a man first achieved a most notable deed he wished to explain to his Tribe what he had done. As soon as he began to speak, however, he was smitten with dumbness, he lacked words, and sat down. Then there arose—according to the story—a masterless man, one who had taken no part in the action of his fellow, who had no special virtues, but who was afflicted—that is the phrase—with the magic of the necessary word. He saw; he told; he described the merits of the notable deed in such a fashion, we are assured, that the words "became alive and walked up and down in the hearts of all his hearers." Thereupon, the Tribe seeing that the words were certainly alive, and fearing lest the man with the words would hand down untrue tales about them to their children, took and killed him. But, later, they saw that the magic was in the words, not in the man.

We have progressed in many directions since the time of this early and destructive criticism, but, so far, we do not seem to have found a sufficient substitute for the necessary word as the final record to which all achievement must look. Even to-day, when all is done, those who have done it must wait until all has been said by the masterless man with the words. It is certain that the overwhelming bulk of those words will perish in the future as they have perished in the past; but it is true that a minute fraction will continue to exist, and by the light of these words, and by that light only, will our children be able to judge of the phases of our generation. Now we desire beyond all things to stand well with our children; but when our story comes to be told we

"Literature," a speech delivered at the Royal Academy Dinner, May 1906. From *A Book of Words* by Rudyard Kipling. Copyright 1928 by Rudyard Kipling. Used by permission of Doubleday, a division of Bantam Doubleday Dell Publishing Group, Inc.

do not know who will have the telling of it. We are too close to the tellers; there are many tellers and they are all talking together; and, even if we know them, we must not kill them. But the old and terrible instinct which taught our ancestors to kill the original story-teller warns us that we shall not be far wrong if we challenge any man who shows signs of being afflicted with the magic of the necessary word. May not this be the reason why, without any special legislation on its behalf, Literature has always stood a little outside the law as the one calling that is absolutely free—free in the sense that it needs no protection? For instance, if, as occasionally happens, a Judge makes a bad law, or a surgeon a bad operation, or a manufacturer makes bad food, criticism upon their actions is by law and custom confined to comparatively narrow limits. But if a man, as occasionally happens, makes a book, there is no limit to the criticism that may be directed against it. And this is perfectly as it should be. The world recognises that little things like bad law, bad surgery, and bad food, affect only the cheapest commodity that we know about—human life. Therefore, in these circumstances, men can afford to be swayed by pity for the offender, by interest in his family, by fear, or loyalty, or respect for the organisation he represents, or even by a desire to do him justice. But when the question is of words—words that may become alive and walk up and down in the hearts of the hearers—it is then that this world of ours, which is disposed to take an interest in its future, feels instinctively that it is better that a thousand innocent people should be punished rather than that one guilty word should be preserved, carrying that which is an untrue tale of the Tribe. The chances, of course, are almost astronomically remote that any given tale will survive for so long as it takes an oak to grow to timber size. But that guiding instinct warns us not to trust to chance a matter of the supremest concern. In this durable record, if anything short of indisputable and undistilled truth be seen there, we all feel, "How shall our achievements profit us?" The Record of the Tribe is its enduring literature.

The magic of Literature lies in the words, and not in any man. Witness, a thousand excellent, strenuous words can leave us quite cold or put us to sleep, whereas a bare half-hundred words breathed upon by some man in his agony, or in his exaltation, or in his idleness, ten generations ago, can still lead whole nations into and out of captivity, can open to us the doors of the three worlds, or stir us so intolerably that we can scarcely abide to look at our own souls. It is a miracle—one that happens very seldom. But secretly each one of the masterless men with the words has hope, or has had hope, that the miracle may be wrought again through him.

And why not? If a tinker in Bedford gaol; if a pamphleteering shop-keeper, pilloried in London; if a muzzy Scot; if a despised German Jew; or a condemned French thief, or an English Admiralty official with a taste for letters can be miraculously afflicted with the magic of the necessary word, why not any man at any time? Our world, which is only concerned in the perpetuation of the record, sanctions that hope just as kindly and just as cruelly as Nature sanctions love.

All it suggests is that the man with the Words shall wait upon the man of achievement, and step by step with him try to tell the story to the Tribe. All it demands is that the magic of every word shall be tried out to the uttermost by every means, fair or foul, that the mind of man can suggest. There is no room, and the world insists that there shall be no room, for pity, for mercy, for respect, for fear, or even for loyalty be-tween man and his fellow-man, when the record of the Tribe comes to be written. That record must satisfy, at all costs to the word and to the man behind the word. It must satisfy alike the keenest vanity and the deepest self-knowledge of the present; it must satisfy also the most shameless curiosity of the future. When it has done this it is literature of which it will be said, in due time, that it fitly represents its age. I say in due time because ages, like individuals, do not always appreci-ate the merits of a record that purports to represent them. The trouble is that one always expects just a little more out of a thing than one puts into it. Whether it be an age or an individual, one is always a little pained and a little pessimistic to find that all one gets back is just one's bare deserts. This is a difficulty old as literature.

A little incident that came within my experience a while ago shows that that difficulty is always being raised by the most unexpected peo-ple all about the world. It happened in a land where the magic of words is peculiarly potent and far-reaching, that there was a Tribe that wanted rain, and the rain-doctors set about getting it. To a certain ex-tent the rain-doctors succeeded. But the rain their magic brought was not a full driving downpour that tells of large prosperity; it was patchy, local, circumscribed, and uncertain. There were unhealthy little squalls blowing about the country and doing damage. Whole districts were flooded out by waterspouts, and other districts annoyed by trickling showers, soon dried by the sun. And so the Tribe went to the rain-doctors, being very angry, and they said, "What is this rain that you make? You did not make rain like this in the time of our fathers. What have you been doing?" And the rain-doctors said, "We have been making our proper magic. Supposing you tell us what you have been doing lately?" And the Tribe said, "Oh, our head-men have been running about hunting jackals, and our little people have been running about chasing grasshoppers! What has that to do with your rain-making?" "It has everything to do with it," said the rain-doctors. "Just as long as your head-men run about hunting jackals, and just as long as your little people run about chasing grasshoppers, just so long will the rain fall in this manner."

"Fiction"

I am sure that to-morrow every member of my craft will be grateful, Lord Balfour, that in your many-sided career you have never thought to compete in the ranks of professed workers in fiction.

As regards the subject, not the treatment, of Lord Balfour's speech, I think we may take it, gentlemen, that the evening light is much the same for all men. When the shadows lengthen one contrasts what one had intended to do in the beginning with what one has accomplished. That the experience is universal does not make it any less acid—especially when, as in my case, one has been extravagantly rewarded for having done what one could not have helped doing.

But recognition by one's equals and betters in one's own craft is a reward of which a man may be unashamedly proud—as proud as I am of the honour that comes to me to-night from your hands. For I know with whom you have seen fit to brigade me in the ranks of Literature. The fiction that I am worthy of that honour be upon your heads!

Yet, at least, the art that I follow is not an unworthy one. For Fiction is Truth's elder sister. Obviously. No one in the world knew what truth was till someone had told a story. So it is the oldest of the arts, the mother of history, biography, philosophy dogmatic (or doubtful, Lord Balfour), and, of course, of politics.

Fiction began when some man invented a story about another man. It developed when another man told tales about a woman. This strenuous epoch begat the first school of destructive criticism, as well as the First Critic, who spent his short but vivid life in trying to explain that a man need not be a hen to judge the merits of an omelette. He died; but the question he raised is still at issue. It was inherited by the earliest writers from their unlettered ancestors, who also bequeathed to them the entire stock of primeval plots and situations—those fifty ultimate comedies and tragedies to which the Gods mercifully limit human action and suffering.

"Fiction," a speech delivered at the Royal Literary Society, June 1926. From *A Book of Words* by Rudyard Kipling. Copyright 1928 by Rudyard Kipling. Used by permission of Doubleday, a division of Bantam Doubleday Dell Publishing Group, Inc.

This changeless aggregate of material workers in fiction through the ages have run into fresh moulds, adorned and adapted to suit the facts and the fancies of their own generation. The Elizabethans, for instance, stood on the edge of a new and wonderful world filled with happy possibilities. Their descendants, 350 years later, have been shot into a world as new and as wonderful, but not quite as happy. And in both ages you can see writers raking the dumps of the English language for words that shall range farther, hit harder, and explode over a wider area than the service-pattern words in common use.

This merciless search, trial, and scrapping of material is one with the continuity of life which, we all know, is as a tale that is told, and which writers feel should be well told. All men are interested in the reflection of themselves and their surroundings, whether in the pure heart of a crystal or in a muddy pool; and nearly every writer who supplies a reflection secretly desires a share of immortality for the pains he has been at in holding up the mirror—which also reflects himself. He may win his desire. Quite a dozen writers have achieved immortality in the past 2500 years. From a bookmaker's—a real bookmaker's—point of view the odds are not attractive, but Fiction is built on fiction. That is where it differs from the other Arts.

Most of the Arts admit the truth that it is not expedient to tell everyone everything. Fiction recognises no such bar. There is no human emotion or mood which it is forbidden to assault—there is no canon of reserve or pity that need be respected—in fiction. Why should there be? The man, after all, is not telling the truth. He is only writing fiction. While he writes it, his world will extract from it just so much of truth or pleasure as it requires for the moment. In time a little more, or much less, of the residue may be carried forward to the general account, and there, perhaps, diverted to ends of which the writer never dreamed.

Take a well-known instance. A man of overwhelming intellect and power goes scourged through life between the dread of insanity and the wrath of his own soul warring with a brutal age. He exhausts mind, heart, and brain in that battle: he consumes himself, and perishes in utter desolation. Out of all his agony remains one little book, his dreadful testament against his fellow-kind, which to-day serves as a pleasant tale for the young under the title of *Gulliver's Travels*. That, and a faint recollection of some baby-talk in some love-letters, is as much as the world has chosen to retain of Jonathan Swift, Master of Irony. Think of it! It is like tuning-down the glare of a volcano to light a child to bed!

The true nature and intention, then, of a writer's work does not lie within his own knowledge. And we know that the world makes little allowance for any glory of workmanship which a writer spends on material that does not interest. So it would seem that Fiction is one of the few "unsheltered" occupations, in that there is equal victimisation on both sides, and no connection between the writer's standard of life, his output, or his wages.

Under these conditions has grown up in England a literature lavish in all aspects—lavish with the inveterate unthrift of the English, who are never happy unless they are throwing things away. By virtue of that same weakness, or strength, it overlaps so sumptuously that one could abstract and bestow from the mere wastage of any literary age since Chaucer's enough of abundance and enjoyment to quicken half a world. Those who study in the treasure-houses of its past know what unregarded perfection of workmanship and what serene independence of design often went to fabricate the least among those treasures. And they know, also, the insolence of the greatest Masters, who were too pressed to wait on perfection in their haste to reveal to us some supreme jewel scarcely cleansed from the matrix. Our English literature, I think, has always been the expression of a race more anxious to deliver what was laid upon it than to measure the means and methods of delivery.

And this immense and profligate range of experience, invention, and passion is our incommunicable inheritance, which is drawn upon at every need, for multitudes who, largely, neither know nor care whence their need is met.

In every age some men gain temporary favour because they happen to have met a temporary need of their age. Yet, as regards their future, they stand on a perfect equality with their fellow-craftsmen. It is not permitted to any generation to know what, or how much, of its effort will be carried forward to the honour and grace of our literature. The utmost a writer can hope is that there may survive of his work a fraction good enough to be drawn upon later, to uphold or to embellish some ancient truth restated, or some old delight reborn.

Admitting this, a man may, by the exercise of a little imagination, persuade himself that he has acquired merit in his lifetime. Or, if imagination be lacking, he may be led to that comfortable conclusion by the magic of his own art heard as we have heard it from Lord Balfour to-night, on the lips of a man wise in life, and a Master not ignorant of the power of words.

Excerpts from *Something of Myself*

. . . Often the night got into my head as it had done in the boarding house in the Brompton Road, and I would wander till dawn in all manner of odd places—liquor-shops, gambling and opium-dens, which are not a bit mysterious, wayside entertainments such as puppet-shows, native dances; or in and about the narrow gullies under the Mosque of Wazir Khan for the sheer sake of looking. Sometimes, the Police would challenge, but I knew most of their officers, and many folk in some quarters knew me for the son of my Father, which in the East more than anywhere else is useful. Otherwise, the word 'Newspaper' sufficed; though I did not supply my paper with many accounts of these prowls. One would come home, just as the light broke, in some night-hawk of a hired carriage which stank of hookah-fumes, jasmine-flowers, and sandalwood; and if the driver were moved to talk, he told one a good deal. Much of real Indian life goes on in the hot weather nights. . . .

This is fit place for a "pivot" experience to be set side by side with the affair of the Adjutant of Volunteers at the Club. It happened one hot-weather evening, in '86 or thereabouts, when I felt that I had come to the edge of all endurance. As I entered my empty house in the dusk there was no more in me except the horror of a great darkness, that I must have been fighting for some days. I came through that darkness alive, but how I do not know. Late at night I picked up a book by Walter Besant which was called *All in a Garden Fair*. It dealt with a young man who desired to write; who came to realise the possibilities of common things seen, and who eventually succeeded in his desire. What its merits may be from today's "literary" standpoint I do not know. But I *do* know that that book was my salvation in sore personal need, and with the reading and re-reading it became to me a revelation, a hope and strength. I was certainly, I argued, as well equipped as the hero and—and—after all, there was no need for me to stay here for ever. I could go away and measure myself against the doorsills of London as soon as I had money. Therefore I would begin to save money, for I perceived there was absolutely no reason outside myself why I should not do exactly what to me seemed good. For proof of my revelation I did, sporadically but sincerely, try to save money, and I built up in my head—always with the book to fall back upon—a dream of the future that sustained me. To Walter Besant singly and solely do I owe this—as I told him when we met, and he laughed, rolled in his chair, and seemed pleased. . . .

My editing of the *Weekly* may have been a shade casual—it was but a re-hash of news and views after all. My head was full of, to me, infinitely more important material. Henceforth no mere twelve-hundred Plain Tales jammed into rigid frames, but three- or five-thousand-word cartoons once a week. So did young Lippo Lippi, whose child I was, look on the blank walls of his monastery when he was bidden decorate them! " 'Twas ask and have, Choose for more's ready," with a vengeance.

I fancy my change of surroundings and outlook precipitated the rush. At the beginning of it I had an experience which, in my innocence, I mistook for the genuine motions of my Daemon. I must have been loaded more heavily than I realised with "Gyp," for there came to me in scenes as stereoscopically clear as those in the crystal an Anglo-Indian *Autour du Mariage*. My pen took charge and I, greatly admiring, watched it write for me far into the nights. The result I christened *The Story of the Gadsbys*, and when it first appeared in England I was complimented on my "knowledge of the world." After my indecent immaturity came to light, I heard less of these gifts. Yet, as the Father said loyally: "It wasn't *all* so dam' bad, Ruddy."

At any rate it went into the *Weekly*, together with soldier tales, Indian tales, and tales of the opposite sex. There was one of this last which, because of a doubt, I handed up to the Mother, who abolished it and wrote me: *Never you do that again.* But I did and managed to pull off, not unhandily, a tale called "A Wayside Comedy," where I worked hard for a certain "economy of implication," and in one phrase of less than a dozen words believed I had succeeded. More than forty years later a Frenchman, browsing about some of my old work, quoted this phrase as the *clou* of the tale and the key to its method. It was a belated "workshop compliment" that I appreciated. Thus, then, I made my own experiments in the weights, colours, perfumes, and attributes of words in relation to other words, either as read aloud so that they may hold the ear, or scattered over the page, draw the eye. There is no line of my verse or prose which has not been mouthed till the tongue has made all smooth, and memory, after many recitals, has mechanically skipped the grosser superfluities. . . .

Most men properly broke to a trade pick up some sort of workshop facility which gives them an advantage over their untrained fellows. My office-work had taught me to think out a notion in detail, pack it away in my head, and work on it by snatches in any surroundings. The lurch and surge of the old horse-drawn buses made a luxurious cradle for such ruminations. Bit by bit, my original notion grew into a vast, vague conspectus—Army and Navy Stores List if you like—of the whole sweep and meaning of things and effort and origins throughout the Empire. I visualised it, as I do most ideas, in the shape of a semicircle of buildings and temples projecting into a sea—of dreams. At any rate, after I had got it straight in my head, I felt there need be no more "knockin' 'em" in the abstract. . . .

I embarked on *Rewards and Fairies*—the second book—in two minds. Stories a plenty I had to tell, but how many would be authentic and how many due to "induction"? There was moreover the old Law: "As soon as you find you can do anything, do something you can't."

My doubt cleared itself with the first tale "Cold Iron," which gave me my underwood: "'What else could I have done?'"—the plinth of all structures. Yet, since the tales had to be read by children, before people realised that they were meant for grown-ups; and since they had to be a sort of balance to, as well as a seal upon, some aspects of my "Imperialistic" output in the past, I worked the material in three or four overlaid tints and textures, which might or might not reveal themselves according to the shifting light of sex, youth, and experience. It was like working lacquer and mother o' pearl, a natural combination, into the same scheme as niello and grisaille, and trying not to let the joins show. . . .

I forget who started the notion of my writing a series of Anglo-Indian tales, but I remember our council over the naming of the series. They were originally much longer than when they appeared, but the shortening of them, first to my own fancy after rapturous re-readings, and next to the space available, taught me that a tale from which pieces have been raked out is like a fire that has been poked. One does not know that the operation has been performed, but every one feels the effect. Note, though, that the excised stuff must have been honestly written for inclusion. I found that when, to save trouble, I "wrote short" *ab initio* much salt went out of the work. This supports the theory of the chimaera which, having bombinated and been removed, *is* capable of producing secondary causes *in vacuo*.

This leads me to the Higher Editing. Take of well-ground Indian Ink as much as suffices and a camel-hair brush proportionate to the inter-spaces of your lines. In an auspicious hour, read your final draft and consider faithfully every paragraph, sentence and word, blacking out where requisite. Let it lie by to drain as long as possible. At the end of that time, re-read and you should find that it will bear a second shortening. Finally, read it aloud alone and at leisure. Maybe a shade more brushwork will then indicate or impose itself. If not, praise Allah and let it go, and "when thou hast done, repent not." The shorter the tale, the longer the brushwork and, normally, the shorter the lie-by, and *vice versa*. The longer the tale, the less brush but the longer lie-by. I have had tales by me for three or five years which shortened themselves almost yearly. The magic lies in the Brush and the Ink. For the Pen, when it is writing, can only scratch; and bottled ink is not to compare with the ground Chinese stick. *Experto crede*. . . .

Let us now consider the Personal Daemon of Aristotle and others, of whom it has been truthfully written, though not published:—

> This is the doom of the Makers—their Daemon lives in their pen.
> If he be absent or sleeping, they are even as other men.
> But if he be utterly present, and they swerve not from his behest,
> The word that he gives shall continue, whether in earnest or jest.

Most men, and some most unlikely, keep him under an alias which varies with their literary or scientific attainments. Mine came to me early when I sat bewildered among other notions, and said: "Take this and no other." I obeyed, and was rewarded. It was a tale in the little Christmas Magazine *Quartette* which we four wrote together, and it was called "The Phantom 'Rickshaw." Some of it was weak, much was bad and out of key; but it was my first serious attempt to think in another man's skin.

After that I learned to lean upon him and recognise the sign of his approach. If ever I held back, Ananias fashion, anything of myself (even though I had to throw it out afterwards) I paid for it by missing what I *then* knew the tale lacked. As an instance, many years later I wrote about a mediaeval artist, a monastery, and the premature discovery of the microscope. ("The Eye of Allah.") Again and again it went dead under my hand, and for the life of me I could not see why. I put it away and waited. Then said my Daemon—and I was meditating something else at the time—"Treat it as an illuminated manuscript." I had ridden off on hard black-and-white decoration, instead of pumicing the whole thing ivory-smooth, and loading it with thick colour and gilt. Again, in a South African, post-Boer War tale called "The Captive," which was built up round the phrase "a first-class dress parade for Armageddon," I could not get my lighting into key with the tone of the monologue. The background insisted too much. My Daemon said at last: "Paint the background first once for all, as hard as a public-house sign, and leave it alone." This done, the rest fell into place with the American accent and outlook of the teller.

My Daemon was with me in the *Jungle Books, Kim,* and both Puck books, and good care I took to walk delicately, lest he should withdraw. I know that he did not, because when those books were finished they said so themselves with, almost, the water-hammer click of a tap turned off. One of the clauses in our contract was that I should never follow up "a success," for by this sin fell Napoleon and a few others. *Note here.* When your Daemon is in charge, do not try to think consciously. Drift, wait, and obey. . . .

In respect to verifying one's references, which is a matter in which one can help one's Daemon, it is curious how loath a man is to take his own medicine. Once, on a Boxing Day, with hard frost coming greasily out of the ground, my friend, Sir John Bland-Sutton, the head of the College of Surgeons, came down to "Bateman's" very full of a lecture which he was to deliver on "gizzards." We were settled before the fire after lunch, when he volunteered that So-and-so had said that if you hold a hen to your ear, you can hear the click in its gizzard of the little pebbles that help its digestion. "Interesting," said I. "He's an authority." "Oh yes, but"—a long pause—"have you any hens about here, Kipling?" I owned that I had, two hundred yards down a lane, but why not accept So-and-so? "I can't," said John simply, "till I've tried it." Remorselessly, he worried me into taking him to the hens, who lived in an open shed in front of the gardener's cottage. As we skated over the glairy ground, I saw an eye at the corner of the drawn-down Boxing-Day blind, and knew that my character for sobriety would be blasted all over the farms before night-fall. We caught an outraged pullet. John soothed her for a while (he said her pulse was a hundred and twenty-six), and held her to his ear. "She clicks all right," he announced. "Listen." I did, and there was click enough for a lecture. "*Now* we can go back to the house," I pleaded. "Wait a bit. Let's catch that cock. He'll click better." We caught him after a loud and long chase, and he clicked like a solitaire-board. I went home, my ears alive with parasites, so wrapped up in my own indignation that the fun of it escaped me. It had not been *my* verification, you see.

But John was right. Take nothing for granted if you can check it. Even though that seem waste-work, and has nothing to do with the essentials of things, it encourages the Daemon. There are always men who by trade or calling know that fact or the inference that you put forth. If you are wrong by a hair in this, they argue. "False in one thing, false in all." Having sinned, I know. Likewise, never play down to your public—not because some of them do not deserve it, but because it is bad for your hand. All your material is drawn from the lives of men.

Part 3

THE CRITICS

Introduction

The rise and fall of Kipling's critical reputation has itself turned into legend. His early stories, though encountering some tepid reviews, were generally applauded; by the time he was twenty-five years old, he had achieved a brilliant success. But, just as quickly it seemed, critics turned against him. He was judged too facile in style, the result of his training in journalism, and, more important, too jingoistic in politics.

A handful of serious readers, T. S. Eliot, Edmund Wilson, Randall Jarrell, reevaluated Kipling's work and, though their judgments may have been mixed, their great contribution may be that they took Kipling seriously as an artist, assumed he was worth exploring, held him to high standards. Still, although he has had an enormous popular following, Kipling has until recently been largely ignored in academic circles. Occasionally a new serious study of his work would appear, J. M. S. Tompkins's *The Art of Rudyard Kipling* or Elliot L. Gilbert's *The Good Kipling,* but for many years it seemed such studies were rare objects, illuminating but isolated.

The past few years have seen, however, a rich production of serious treatments of Kipling's work. Representing a variety of approaches, willing to find both strengths and weaknesses, these new studies may not ignore Kipling's subject matter or temperament, but they admit the complexity of his work, recognize that the views his characters speak are filtered through an often ambiguous narrative voice, that the patterns of imagery or ironic overstatement may make untenable an easy assumption that Kipling's treatment of ideas is univocal. And they have concentrated as well on a variety of stories that have hitherto been neglected.

John A. McClure's *Kipling and Conrad: The Colonial Fiction* tackles the vexing problem of Kipling's politics by approaching the stories in a psychological and social context. In his discussion of "The Return of Imray," McClure reveals Kipling's subtle portrayal of the precarious mental and moral position Empire builders found themselves in.

Clare Hanson's *Short Stories and Short Fictions, 1880–1980* approaches Kipling's work as part of the development of the short story. She focuses on the structure and technique of Kipling's stories both as they reveal his growth as a writer and as they exhibit his connections to other practitioners of the genre.

John A. McClure

. . . Kipling looks on the imperialists' plunge into the little world of the club with considerable anxiety. For those characters in his stories who have ventured beyond the commonplace, the club provides little solace; meanwhile it keeps other men from standing firm with their more exposed comrades. Ignorant of India, and addicted to the false security provided by the club, most imperialists are unwilling to take the dangerous but essential step from "the commonplace" to "the horrible." Thus Kipling's genuine appreciation of the distracting and identity-confirming rituals of the club coexists with a recognition that dependence on these rituals only increases the imperialist's vulnerability. This insight is dramatized vividly in "The Return of Imray" (1890).

The three main characters are Imray, an imperial official who has recently disappeared, Strickland, an officer in the imperial police now living in Imray's bungalow, and the narrator, who is staying with Strickland while visiting the district. The story opens with a brief description of the missing Imray. The narrator stresses Imray's conventionality; prior to his disappearance his entire world was the little English community of the station where he lived, and he spent much of his time at the heart of this community, "among the billiard-tables at his Club."[1] For this reason, his disappearance is doubly mysterious.

Strickland's unconventional ways make him Imray's opposite. A favorite Kipling hero in the early stories, Strickland is introduced as a character whom the reader may already know. The narrator alludes specifically to episodes in Strickland's adventurous life, which are chronicled in "Miss Youghal's Sais" (1887) and "The Mark of the Beast" (1890), tales that deal with Strickland's exploits as a master of Indian customs, a cunning impersonator, and a fearless policeman. In spite of his successes, however, Strickland's "investigations into native life" are frowned upon, as are his eccentric domestic habits. The narrator observes that the police officer's "life was sufficiently pecu-

Reprinted by permission of the publishers from *Kipling and Conrad: The Colonial Fiction* by John A. McClure, Cambridge, Mass.: Harvard University Press. Copyright ©1981 by the President and Fellows of Harvard College.

liar, and men complained of his manners and customs" (p. 285). Thus while Imray is portrayed as a model of propriety, Strickland is introduced as a man who meets with disapproval from the members of his own community. Imray relies on the club; Strickland scorns it. Which man, the story asks, should actually command respect and emulation?

The narrator acts as arbiter in resolving this central question. His personality suits him for this role: he knows and admires Strickland, but has a great deal in common with Imray. Their similarity is revealed when the narrator discovers that Strickland's bungalow is haunted: "I explained to Strickland, gently as might be, that I would go over to the Club and find for myself quarters there. I admired his hospitality, was pleased with his guns and rods, but I did not much care for his house and its atmosphere" (p. 292). Strickland opposes this retreat into the conventional in words that have a particular weight of meaning for Kipling: "Stay on . . . and see what this thing means" (p. 292). But the narrator's concern is precisely not to see, and he steadfastly refuses to remain overnight. His instinct, like Imray's, is to seek refuge from mystery within the commonplace world of the club.

The narrator does agree, however, to spend the evening with Strickland, and in the course of his stay the mystery is solved. As events unfold, the dissimilarities between the narrator's responses to the unknown and Strickland's become more and more apparent. When two snakes crawl up into the atticlike space between the ceiling-cloth and the thatched roof, Strickland ignores the narrator's warnings and pursues them. Searching for the snakes, he discovers a bundled object resting on a roof beam. He pushes the mysterious object off onto the ceiling-cloth and its rips through, falling into the room where the narrator is waiting. Once again, the narrator retreats from vision. The bundle lands in front of him. "I dared not look . . . till Strickland . . . was standing by my side" (p. 295). The bundle contains the body of Imray, who, Strickland determines, has been murdered by his servant.

Strickland's boldness enables him to solve a murder that the timid narrator would never even have detected. His victory suggests that other imperial servants must be ready to expose themselves to the threatening world beyond the club and the station. Indeed, the story suggests that such exposure is essential to survival. As it turns out, Imray was killed as a result of an ignorant act of goodwill. He complimented his servant's son, a gesture considered the same as a curse by the boy's people. When the child died of fever, the father killed Imray in revenge. Kipling makes sure that the implications of this tragic misunderstanding won't be lost on his readers: " 'Imray made a mistake.' 'Simply and solely through not knowing the nature of the Oriental . . . Bahadur Khan had been with him for four years' " (p. 302). Imray's retreat from exposure to India leaves him fatally ignorant and vulnerable. In contrast, Strickland's habits, for which he is criticized by men like Imray, keep him and the community alive. The immediate political theme is clear: the ignorance fostered by the club represents a dangerous foundation for rule.

In the end, the narrator of "The Return of Imray" signifies his acceptance of this warning by staying on with Strickland in the house of the murdered Imray. But the narrator's close resemblance to the dead man is stressed once again in the final paragraphs of the story. When Strickland observes that Imray's servant had been with him for four years, the narrator is startled: "I shuddered. My own servant had been with me for exactly that length of time" (p. 302).

This insistent identification of the two men coincides with other elements in "The Return of Imray" to invite an interpretation of the story as a loosely constructed psychological allegory. Other aspects of the story that point to this kind of a reading are the vivid and detailed descriptions of the house itself, of the narrator's inexplicable fears, and of the sudden appearance of Imray's body.

Early in the story the reader's attention is directed to the dark and mysterious area of the bungalow just under the roof. "Under the pitch of the roof ran a ceiling-cloth which looked just as neat as a whitewashed ceiling. The landlord had repainted it when Strickland took the bungalow. Unless you knew how Indian bungalows were built you would never have suspected that above the cloth lay the dark three-cornered cavern of the roof, where the beams and the underside of the thatch harboured all manner of rats, bats, ants, and foul things" (p. 287). Among the "foul things" hidden away in this carefully screened-off realm is the body of Imray, whose ghost, like an unacknowledged fear, so frightens the narrator in the room below. In contrast to the narrator, Strickland is not afraid. Like a modern-day psychoanalyst, he fearlessly explores the dark world that is the source of the narrator's fears, while the narrator himself remains below, insisting on his total ignorance of what lies above while, at the same time, manifesting an inordinate degree of anxiety. "I set my teeth and lifted the rod," he recalls, "for I had not the least knowledge of what might descend" (p. 294).

When Imray's body falls, the narrator experiences the event as a traumatic psychological breakthrough, the emergence into consciousness of some hitherto repressed terror. The mysterious object breaks through the fragile barrier of cloth with a terrible, dreamlike slowness and inexorability: "I saw the ceiling-cloth nearly in the centre of the room bag with a shape that was pressing it downwards and downwards towards the lighted lamp on the table. I snatched the lamp out of danger and stood back. Then the cloth ripped out from the walls, tore, split, swayed, and shot down upon the table something that I dared not look at till Strickland had slid down the ladder and was standing by my side." (p. 295). Why does the narrator experience the event in this way; why is he so terrified by the bundle that he dares not face it? The reiterated identification of the narrator with Imray provides a possible answer. Perhaps Imray's body, like the terrible apparition that forces its way into Hummil's vision in "At the End of the Passage," represents the narrator's own repressed self-image, an image of himself as a potential victim of forces beyond his knowledge.

Indeed, Kipling's descriptions of madness during this period often involve the breakthrough of sinister forces from a realm of outer darkness. The narrator of "The Phantom Rickshaw" explains Pansay's death with the theory "that there was a crack in Pansay's head and a little bit of the Dark World came through and pressed him to death."[2] Although Hummil's madness in "At the End of the Passage" is attributed to his having fallen into the "Dark Places,"[3] the fact that the ceiling-cloth of his bungalow is torn is mentioned twice. But while for Pansay and Hummil the breakthroughs prove fatal, the narrator in "The Return of Imray" is cured of his terror by the appearance of Imray. This is true, however, only because Strickland is there to confront his fears with him, to provide a logical explanation of their source, and to offer a prescription for their permanent banishment.

The allegorical and literal elements of the story merge at this point. Kipling is concerned to show that the narrator's fear is somewhat irrational, and his reaction to that fear totally so. Imray's ghost, which has plagued the narrator, is in one sense of projection of his own fears. But it is a projection founded on an actual murder—Imray and thousands of other imperial servants have been killed in India. These murders, Kipling suggests, provide the fertile soil in which the fears of living imperialists can flourish. Thus the images of men actually killed in India find their ways into the unconsciousness of their living fellows, where they survive as foreshadowings of potential doom. The flight to the club results from this combination of real dangers and imagined horrors.

What Strickland shows the narrator is that his future need not be Imray's, that the dreams that haunt his sleep do not depict an inevitable doom. Imray, he insists, died because he was ignorant; his death could have been avoided. Only if the narrator follows Imray's course and withdraws into the club is he likely to meet his fate. Kipling's theme here is clear: he invites the imperial servant to become more familiar with the Indian community, and he argues that the fear preventing exploration of that community is the imperialist's greatest enemy.

Notes

McClure states that he is using the Outward Bound Edition, 30 volumes (New York: Charles Scribner's Sons, 1897–1923).

1. Rudyard Kipling, "The Return of Imray," in Phantom Rickshaw, p. 284. Subsequent references to this edition appear in the text.

2. Kipling, "Phantom Rickshaw," p. 3.

3. Kipling, "End of the Passage," p. 37.

Part 3

Clare Hanson

. . . The anecdote relies for its effect on convention. It both appeals to and endorses a shared system of values: at its simplest level it appears as the "in joke" and it may have a certain bravura quality, affirming group values a shade too emphatically. It will normally be told by a first-person narrator who guarantees both the tale and certain values associated with it.

The anecdote informs some of the early work of Kipling, who projects, as many critics have noted, a rather irritatingly knowing air in some of the stories of *Plain Tales from the Hills*. This could be referred to a need to over-compensate, to affirm absolutely one's place in a society where there are no absolutes. In stories of his middle and later periods, however, Kipling moved from anecdotal to mythical and fantastic modes. In an age of experiment in the short story form one would expect a writer such as Kipling, acknowledged as a master of the genre by the time he was thirty, to experiment widely. Among Kipling's later work we find many different types of short story: proto-science fiction ("As Easy as A.B.C."); stories influenced by cinema technique ("Mrs Bathurst," "My Son's Wife"); fables *à la* La Fontaine ("The Mother Hive"); more importantly, stories of the supernatural ("They," "The Wish House," "A Madonna of the Trenches"); also complex Jamesian studies of manners and motive ("Mary Postgate," "Dayspring Mishandled").

In his elliptical autobiography *Something of Myself* (1937) Kipling wrote of his early discovery in writing *Plain Tales from the Hills* that

> a tale from which pieces have been raked out is like a fire that has been poked. One does not know that the operation has been performed, but everyone feels the effect. Note, though, that the excised stuff must have been honestly written for inclusion. I found that when, to save trouble, I "wrote short" *ab initio* much salt went out of the work.[1]

Kipling's description of his "cutting" technique is illuminating. It suggests that he was in essence a "metonymic" writer, first forming his narratives according to the "law of combination along the axis of contiguity,"[2] only subsequently cutting what seemed least expres-sive, in a symbolic sense, of his central theme. In consequence Kipling's stories often have lacunae which make them seem elliptical in a modernist manner. His stories have been described as modernist,[3] but this is inaccurate. The ellipses in the works of the modernists generally occur for an "opposite" reason, when the author is combining the elements of his story according to the law of similarity, not contiguity, and sacrifices narrative continuity to symbolic order. The basic trope of the modernist story is metaphor, while Kipling's stories often centre around a synecdoche or metonymy, for example Bisesa's "roseleaf hands" in "Beyond the Pale" or Holden's Indian home in "Without Benefit of Clergy," whose desolation at the close of the story mirrors a man's state of mind: "He found that the rains had torn down the mud pillars of the gateway, and the heavy wooden gate that had guarded his life hung lazily from one hinge."[4]

Stories with a plot tend to deal with limits and extremes of situation and human behaviour. In the case of Stevenson a fascination with the extreme signifies a desire to push beyond "normal" states of being and to interrogate the concept of humanity. In Kipling's work an equally strong tendency to the extreme appears to stem from a desire to push to its limits the code of behaviour within which the "real" author had been brought up. Kipling opposes this code to a bizarre or horrifying situation and dispassionately watches it crack, without, in the early stories, offering anything in its place. In the work written after 1900, he offers a sense of place as a corrective to breakdown and loss of the self. This trend is illustrated by two stories, one of 1904 and one of 1913. They furnish examples of the extraordinary unevenness of Kipling's work and offer a focal point for discussion of the "flawed" quality of his writing.

"My Son's Wife" is the later of the two. The title immediately suggests a sense of possession, relationship and security, and this is a sense which gradually envelops the hero as the story progresses. The title phrase is sung by a woman who will become the protagonist's wife: it acts as the opening phrase for a new movement in his life. The story is a parable turning on the regeneration of the hero as he abandons town life and socialism—apparently inextricably linked—in favour of the countryside and conservative social values. Midmore changes from a man who had "attached himself to the Immoderate Left" into a country squire possessed by the idea of possession:

> Everything his eyes opened upon was his very own to keep for ever. The carved four-post Chippendale bed, obviously worth hundreds; the wavy walnut William and Mary chairs—he had seen worse ones labelled twenty guineas apiece; the oval medallion mirror; the delicate eighteenth-century wire fireguard; the heavily brocaded curtains were his—all his.[5]

Vulgar materialism and an easy satire which takes the place of political understanding are apparent in this story. Moreover there is an over-assertiveness in some of the phrasing which seems to indicate a writer only half at ease with his material:

> Such pagan delights as these were followed by pagan sloth of evenings. . . . But Midmore preferred to lie out on a yellow silk couch, reading works of a debasing vulgarity; or, by invitation, to dine with the Sperrits and savages of their kidney.[6]

The over-insistent "Englishness" of this passage suggests an observer writing of an alien culture, anxious to learn the rules and passwords which will make him acceptable within it. This strain—in both senses of the word—is there in Kipling, and yet ten years earlier he had recorded in "They" a most delicate appreciation of English country life. "They," of course, influenced T. S. Eliot in the writing of "Burnt Norton." In this story Kipling achieved the sure grasp of specific place and time which Eliot was later to prescribe for the "intersection of the timeless moment" with time—"In England and nowhere."

"They" opens with a sweeping panorama of the Sussex countryside, which gradually closes in on the narrator and the reader. The form of a quest is embedded in the successive stages of the narrative, which leads the reader on as in a maze:

> One view called me to another; one hill-top to its fellow, half across the country . . .
> I found hidden villages where bees, the only things awake, boomed in eighty-foot lindens . . .
> I did not allow for the confusing veils of the woods. A quick turn plunged me first into a green cutting brim-full of liquid sunshine.[7]

The rich, atmospheric description is on an imaginative level quite different from that of "My Son's Wife." In "They" the country house has full weight in the text, functioning as an image of accommodation between the forces of nature and of history:

> As the light beat across my face my fore-wheels took the turf of a great still lawn from which sprang horsemen ten feet high with levelled lances. . . . Across the lawn—the marshalled woods besieged it on three sides—stood an ancient house of lichened and weather-worn stone, with mullioned windows and roofs of rose-red tile. It was flanked by semi-circular walls, also rose-red, that closed the lawn on the fourth side, and at their feet a box hedge grew man-high. There were doves on the roofs about the slim brick chimneys.[8]

"They" is a story of the supernatural, and some critics have complained of its realistic social and physical setting which, they feel, jars with the supernatural elements of the tale. Yet one could argue that the intermeshing of the two is Kipling's precarious achievement. Motor cars and Ordnance Survey maps offer one way of approaching the house and its mysterious inhabitants but on an intersecting plane is the narrator's sighting of the ghost children in the wood and by the fountain; a sighting possible only for those who have themselves lost a child. The mingling of the two levels of "reality" offers a triumph of control of tone:

> It was a long afternoon crowded with mad episodes that rose and dissolved like the dust of our wheels; cross-sections of remote and incomprehensible lives through which we raced at right angles; and I went home in the dusk, wearied out, to dream of the clashing horns of the cattle; round-eyed nuns walking in a garden of graves; pleasant tea-parties beneath shady trees, the carbolic-scented, grey-painted corridors of the County Institute; the steps of shy children in the wood, and the hands that clung to my knees as the motor began to move.[9]

"They" covers in the space of a few pages several weeks in time and a variety of incidents but the diverse elements of the story are held together by the presence of a characteristically static narrative voice, heavily adjectival and with few active verbs, creating a single "time of narrative."

A progression is discernible in Kipling's work from a youthful sense of *nada* and existential despair to a defining of the self through a sense of place which in turn makes possible the development of certain areas of the spiritual life. The intermeshing of levels of the "real" and supernatural is perhaps Kipling's greatest contribution to the short story form. His metonymic cutting technique, akin to that of a film editor, forges stories which are fluid and restless in structure, never able to rest on a single perspective on reality and thus susceptible to the incorporation of elements of the supernatural and surreal.

The category of the supernatural needs a little more definition. It enters a significant number of Kipling's stories after 1900. In some cases he does no more than toy with fairly trite and superficial ideas of spiritualism or telepathy, in "Wireless" for example and "A Madonna of the Trenches." In neither of these stories does the supernatural have any status in itself: it remains a curiosity and has no integral connection with the development of the tale. However in many of the finer stories (including "They"), the use of the supernatural adds an extra dimension to the tale while contributing to thematic development. The introduction of something felt as alien to human experience throws into relief the normal, what is deep and enduring in human life.

The supernatural relates to things which cannot be explained by natural law, and by extension from this the term is used to refer to events caused either by a god or by occult beings. The term is used more loosely to denote simply that which exceeds the ordinary, i.e. the abnormal. The last is the sense most pertinent here. Though references to the occult and to the suspension of natural law occur frequently in the short story, they function in literary terms primarily as metaphors directing us to a sense of the strange or abnormal—they are not usually intended to be taken literally. The device of the "wish house" in Kipling's story of that name functions like this.

The literature of the supernatural has its specialised vocabulary, which is a vocabulary of negation. The writer will frequently refer to the un-natural, the un-earthly, the in-tangible, the in-visible; also to the un-speakable, the un-utterable, the un-imaginable. The second category directs our attention to the idea of a potential which is sensed beyond the familiar areas of experience charted by language.

"The Wish House" (1924) fruitfully entwines natural and supernatural elements. The story is built on a fundamental contrast between the natural and supernatural, between the superstitious beliefs of the elderly women characters and their attitude to these beliefs. Grace Ashcroft, the main speaker of the story, believes that she has taken on herself all the hurt which would otherwise have fallen on the man she loved. This has been achieved by means of the "wish house," which she first heard about from a little girl who claimed to have "taken away" her headache:

> Sophy said there was a Wish 'Ouse in Wadloes Road—just a few streets off, on the way to our green-grocer's. All you 'ad to do, she said, was to ring the bell an' wish your wish through the slit o' the letter-box.[10]

The wish is granted by "a Token," a wraith of the dead or the living, but, we are told, "All you'll get at a Wish 'Ouse is leave to take some one else's trouble"—you cannot ask for anything for yourself. Grace Ashcroft has asked to take "everythin' bad that's in store for my man . . . for love's sake," and since that time has traced a relation between the health and welfare of her ex-lover and the state of a sick leg she has had from the day she visited the wish house. Now she senses that she has not long to live, but insists that she wants no more than she has had from life. As long as "de pain is taken into de reckonin," as long as she has kept Harry well at her expense, Grace is content. Her feeling stems from a realistic mixture of motives, in part altruistic, in part fiercely possessive—Grace wishes to feel that in taking on Harry's pain she has possessed him as no one else can. This mixture of motives fits in well with the down-to-earth, physical nature of her love for Harry: "I couldn't ever get 'Arry—'ow *could* I? I knowed it must go on burnin' till it burned me out."[11] Throughout the story the elements of the uncanny are so deployed as to sharpen the reader's sense of the strongly and deeply human in the characters of the two elderly women speakers. The wish house itself is clearly uncanny, *unheimlich*—a suburbanised version of the deserted Gothic castle of earlier fiction:

> Fourteen, Wadloes Road, was the place—a liddle basement-kitchen 'ouse, in a row of twenty–thirty such, and tiddy strips o' walled garden in front—the paint off the front door, an' na'undone to na'un since ever so long. There wasn't 'ardly no one in the streets 'cept the cats. *'Twas* 'ot, too! I turned into the gate bold as brass; up de steps I went and' I ringed the front-door bell. She

pealed loud, like it do in an empty house. When she'd all ceased, I
'eard a cheer, like, pushed back on de floor o' the kitchen.[12]

The apprehension of something inhuman is powerfully conveyed
through the tone and vocabulary of Grace Ashcroft's speaking voice.
Her voice is skilfully exploited as a narrative device: because Grace
believes implicitly in the story she is telling, she convinces us. Para-
doxically it is her acceptance of the uncanny which makes it possible
for us to believe in it on one narrative level and makes us question it
on another. For Grace's vivid maturity, her quality of acceptance,
dominates the story, dwarfing the invocations of household ghosts and
"Tokens." It is a maturity which is eminently natural, as Kipling
stresses by repeatedly linking Grace and her natural environment:

> Mrs Ashcroft shook her head slowly—she never hurried—and went
> on stitching a sack-cloth lining into a list-bound rush tool-basket.
> Mrs Fettley laid out more patches in the spring light through the
> geraniums on the window-sill, and they were silent awhile.[13]

> A couple of jays squealed and skirmished through the undraped ap-
> ple-trees in the garden. This time, the word was with Mrs Ashcroft,
> her elbows on the tea-table, and her sick leg propped on a stool.[14]

It is uncanny for the reader to hear Mrs Ashcroft detailing the connections between her bad leg and Harry's illnesses:

> "That day," Mrs Ashcroft went on, "I'd stood on me feet nigh all
> the time, watching the doctor go in an' out; for they thought it
> might be 'is ribs, too. That made my boil break again, issuin' an'
> weeping. But it turned out 'twadn't ribs at all and 'Arry 'ad a good
> night. . . . It didn't hurt me that day, to speak of—seemed more to
> draw the strength out o' me like—and 'Arry 'ad another good night.
> That made me persevere. . . ."[15]

But Grace Ashcroft does not find it uncanny. It is natural for human
beings to want to make sacrifices for those they love, and natural for
them to make some sort of connection between pain which they suffer
and some reward, either in this life or the next. Her attitude is simply
the most positive we can adopt in the face of human suffering—"It *do*
count, don't it—de pain?"

The delicacy of "The Wish House" is due in large part to Kipling's deft handling of the dialogue through which the story is conveyed. Mrs Ashcroft and Mrs Fettley speak "precisely" in "deep tones" and a contrapuntal effect is achieved through a stylistic trick of each speaker's picking up one of the closing words of the other:

> "Nothin' was *said* to ye?" Mrs Fettley demanded.
> "Na'un. She just breathed out—a sort of *A-ah*, like." [16]

In structuring the story Kipling used cinematic cutting techniques with consummate skill. In snatches of dialogue the two women manage to reveal all the significant episodes of their lives, in a kind of montage effect. In less than twenty pages the life-span of the two women is covered, with no sense of artifice or strain. The story gives the impression of being finely honed: the art is primarily one of nicely judged omission. For example, Mrs Fettley's story is inferred from the closing lines of her recital, which are all that are given:

> Mrs Fettley had spoken very precisely for some time without inter-ruption, before she wiped her eyes. "And," she concluded, "they read 'is death-notice to me, out o' the paper last month. O' course it wadn't any o' *my* becomin' concerns—let be I 'adn't set eyes on him for so long." [17]

Like other Kipling stories "The Wish House" is indeed like a hugely truncated novel. It is quite characteristic of his work that he does not deal with single episodes, normally thought to be the staple of the story-teller, but deals elliptically with large and complex narra-tives, often covering a long time-span and involving many characters.

One of his very late stories, "Dayspring Mishandled," offers one of the most intriguing examples of this elliptical method. The theme is Jamesian and the story operates on multiple levels of ambiguity. The "dayspring mishandled" of the title refers to the youth, energy, talent and ability to love of the two young men who are at the centre of the story. They come together, as a result of lack of opportunities in the higher echelons of literature, to work for a financially rewarding "Fic-tional Supply Syndicate." In the course of time, one, Castorley, be-comes a well-known literary critic; the other, Manallace, continues to produce hackwork, but earns enough money by it to support a woman whom he and Castorley have both loved. The lives of the two men continue to intertwine over the years, until a decisive evening when Castorley says something unforgivable about the woman involved. Manallace then devises an intricate plot to bring about the other man's downfall. He forges a Chaucer manuscript which Castorley "discovers" and acclaims, subsequently receiving a title for his services to literature. It was Manallace's intention then to expose him, and he has merely been waiting for the appropriate moment. But Castorley's wife has not only guessed the truth about the manuscript but is even more anxious for her husband's downfall than is his erstwhile friend. The latter thus finds himself in a dilemma. He sees that the wife's cruelty, which is abhorrent to his sensibility, is merely a magnified image of his own, and he becomes more and more loath to put his plan of unmasking and revenge into action. In the end he becomes involved in a struggle with the wife to put off the day of revelation. Only with Castorley's death does he become safe, as the wife prepares happily to marry her lover, the dead man's surgeon.

The portrait of Castorley is an engaging, if slightly scathing, one of a literary critic complete with affected, slightly "gamy," 'ninetyish speech:

> The freshness, the fun, the humanity, the fragrance of it all, cries—no, shouts—itself as Dan's work. Why 'Daiespringe mishandled' alone stamps it from Dan's mint. Plangent as doom, my dear boy—plangent as doom![18]

The portrait of Manallace is a study in obsession, an obsession which has acted as a displacement activity distracting him from failures in private and public life. The painstakingly detailed plot against Castorley and the hatred nurtured over years are both misplaced uses of energy, as Manallace realises at the close of the story when he also realises that he will be unable to "redeem the time" he has wasted.

Waste of time and life are the major themes of the story, and are nowhere more sharply expressed than at the moment when Manallace sees his revenge turn back on itself, as he first sees the ugly image of his hatred in the wife of his colleague. He sees the futility of the purpose which has been for years his *raison d'être*. This moment is at the centre of the spider's web of the narrative of "Dayspring Mishandled." The narrative is elliptical and tortuous, a complex narrative order mirroring a slow process of self-discovery for Manallace.

Castorley reflects towards the close of "Dayspring Mishandled": "Life had always been one long innuendo." The phrase doesn't quite fit our usual image of Kipling but it is suggestive in connection with his later work. Kipling's technique here is precisely one of innuendo. He did not fall into the trap of increased prolixity with the increased complexity of his subject matter but continually refined on the expressive substance of his stories while observing the need for verbal brevity in the short form. Sean O'Faolain has described the "eloquence of form" which resulted, and, interestingly, singles out James as an example of a contemporary who failed to achieve such formal eloquence, who "sprawled" in a manner unacceptable for the abbreviated form. The comparison is revealing, throwing into a sharper focus the special nature of Kipling's achievement.

Notes

1. Rudyard Kipling, Something of Myself (1937), p. 207.
2. See Roman Jakobson, "Two Aspects of Language and Two Types of Aphasic Disturbances," in Fundamentals of Language, ed. R. Jakobson and M. Halle (The Hague, 1956), pp. 52–82.
3. For example by Walter Allen in The Short Story in English (Oxford, 1981), p. 72.
4. Rudyard Kipling, Life's Handicap: Being Stories of Mine Own People (1918), p. 181.
5. Rudyard Kipling, Short Stories, vol. 2, Penguin edn. (Harmondsworth, 1971), p. 29.
6. Ibid., p. 41.
7. Rudyard Kipling, Short Stories, vol. 1, Penguin edn. (Harmondsworth, 1971), p. 93.
8. Ibid., p. 94.
9. Ibid., p. 107.
10. Kipling, Short Stories, vol. 2, p. 172.
11. Ibid., p. 175.
12. Ibid., p. 175.
13. Ibid., p. 163.
14. Ibid., p. 167.
15. Ibid., pp. 177–78.
16. Ibid., p. 176.
17. Ibid., p. 167.
18. Ibid., p. 221.

Chronology

1865	Rudyard Kipling born 30 December to John Lockwood and Alice Kipling in Bombay.
1871–1877	At "Lorne Lodge," Southsea.
1878–1882	At United Services College, Devon.
1882–1887	On the staff of the *Civil and Military Gazette*, Lahore.
1885	"The Strange Ride of Morrowbie Jukes" and "The Phantom 'Rickshaw" published in *Quartette*, the Christmas annual of the *Civil and Military Gazette*.
1886	*Departmental Ditties.* Andrew Lang reviews, the first review of any work by Kipling in England.
1887–1889	On the staff of the *Pioneer*, Allahabad.
1888	*Plain Tales from the Hills.* "Indian Railway Library" editions: *Soldiers Three, The Story of the Gadsbys, In Black and White, Under the Deodars, The Phantom 'Rickshaw, Wee Willie Winkie.*
1889	Leaves India for England.
1890	*The Light that Failed, Barrack-Room Ballads.*
1891	*Letters of Marque, American Notes, Life's Handicap.*
1892	Marries Caroline Balestier, settles in Brattleboro, Vermont. Daughter Josephine born.
1893	*Many Inventions.*
1894	*The Jungle Book.*
1895	*The Second Jungle Book.*
1896	Daughter Elsie born. Returns to live in England.
1897	Son, John, born. *Captains Courageous.* "Recessional" published in the London *Times*.
1898	*The Day's Work.*

1899 Josephine dies. Kipling offered a knighthood, declines. *Stalky & Co., From Sea to Sea.*

1900 In Cape Town, writes for newspapers on the Boer War.

1901 *Kim* serialized.

1902 Settles at "Bateman's" in Sussex. *Just So Stories.*

1903 Offered a Knight Commander of the Order of St. Michael and St. George, declines.

1904 *Traffics and Discoveries.*

1906 *Puck of Pook's Hill.*

1907 Awarded Nobel Prize for Literature. *Collected Verse.* Accepts doctorates from Universities of Durham, Oxford.

1908 Accepts doctorate from University of Cambridge.

1909 *Actions and Reactions.*

1910 *Rewards and Fairies.*

1912–1913 *Songs from Books.*

1915 John is killed. Accepts appointment as member of the Imperial War Graves Commission.

1917 *A Diversity of Creatures.*

1919 *The Years Between.*

1920 Accepts doctorate from University of Edinburgh. *Letters of Travel.*

1921 Accepts doctorates from Universities of Paris and Strasbourg.

1923 *Land and Sea Tales.* Elected Lord Rector of St. Andrews. *The Irish Guards in the Great War* (2 vols.).

1924 Declines, for the second time, Order of Merit.

1926 *Debits and Credits.* Receives Gold Medal of Royal Society of Literature.

1928 *A Book of Words.*

1932 *Limits and Renewals.* Elected Honorary Fellow, Magdalen College, Cambridge.

1933 *Souvenirs of France.*

1935 Begins *Something of Myself.* Numerous films of works: *Kim, Captains Courageous, Light that Failed, Toomai of the Elephants* (later called *Elephant Boy*), *Soldiers Three.*

1936 Dies 18 January. Cremated. Ashes interred in Poets' Corner, Westminster Abbey.

1937 *Something of Myself*, edited by Carrie Kipling.

1937–1939 *The Sussex Edition* (35 vols). Complete edition of acknowledged works, many previously uncollected; prepared by Kipling.

1940 *Rudyard Kipling's Verse: Definitive Edition*.

Selected Bibliography

Primary Works

The following is not a complete bibliography of Kipling's work. He was a writer both prolific and peripatetic, and his publishing history is extremely complex. His earliest stories were published in one or the other of the two Anglo-Indian newspapers for which he wrote; some of these stories were later published in pamphlet form for the Indian Railway Library, as the name suggests, an inexpensive, traveler's format. Throughout his life, he regularly published his stories first in magazines, later in collections.

Copyright was a major problem for authors in Kipling's day. Some of his stories and poems were printed without his permission, and he disclaimed such editions. But many of them existed, in a variety of languages and multitude of formats. Kipling often hurried an edition to print in order to secure the copyright. And he permitted numerous new editions that might include mostly reprints of stories or poems and one or two new items.

In the following bibliography, I list the first collected edition of the short stories, omitting pirated and unauthorized editions and those that include only one or two new works. To make locating these stories in modern editions easier, I indicate the names of the collections in which these stories finally appear in the thirty-five-volume Sussex Edition, the standard library edition and model for most contemporary collections (London: Macmillan and Co. Ltd., 1937–39). For ease of citing material within my text, I also include the abbreviation I use for each short-story collection.

Compiling a bibliography for Kipling's other writing presents the same difficulties. Much of his poetry and nonfiction appeared first in magazines, newspaper articles, letters to the editor, or speeches. Here too I list the first authorized collected edition of these works. Uncollected material, fiction, nonfiction, and poetry, can be found in the Sussex Edition.

For those who wish further information on Kipling's bibliography, the standard, indispensible work is James McGregor Stewart's *Rudyard Kipling: A Bibliographical Catalogue*, edited by A. W. Yeats (Toronto: Dalhousie University Press, 1959).

Collections of Short Stories

Actions and Reactions (*A&R*). London: Macmillan and Co., Limited, 1909. "An Habitation Enforced," "Garm—A Hostage," "The Mother Hive," "With the Night Mail," "A Deal in Cotton," "The Puzzler," "Little Foxes," "The House Surgeon."

The Day's Work (*DW*). New York: Doubleday & McClure Co., 1898. "The Bridge-Builders," "A Walking Delegate," "The Ship that Found Herself," "The Tomb of His Ancestors," "The Devil and the Deep Sea," "William the Conqueror," "—007," "The Maltese Cat," " 'Bread upon the Waters,' " "An Error in the Fourth Dimension," "My Sunday at Home," "The Brushwood Boy."

Debits and Credits (*D&C*). London: Macmillan and Co., Ltd., 1926. "The Enemies to Each Other," "Sea Constables," "In the Interest of the Brethren," "The United Idolators," "The Wish House," "The Janeites," "The Prophet and the Country," "The Bull that Thought," "A Madonna of the Trenches," "The Propagation of Knowledge," "A Friend of the Family," "On the Gate: A Tale of '16," "The Eye of Allah," "The Gardener."

A Diversity of Creatures (*ADC*). London: Macmillan and Co., Ltd., 1917. "As Easy as A.B.C.," "Friendly Brook," "In the Same Boat," "The Honours of War," "The Dog Hervey," "The Village that Voted the Earth Was Flat," "In the Presence," "Regulus," "The Edge of the Evening," "The Horse Marines," "My Son's Wife," "The Vortex," "Swept and Garnished," "Mary Postgate."

In Black and White (*B&W*). Allahabad: A. H. Wheeler & Co., 1888. Later collected in *Soldiers Three*. "Dray Wara Yow Dee," "The Judgment of Dungara," "A Howli Thana," "Gemini," "At Twenty-Two," "In Flood Time," "The Sending of Dana Da," "On the City Wall."

The Jungle Book (*JB*). London: Macmillan and Co., 1894. "Mowgli's Brothers," "Kaa's Hunting," " 'Tiger-Tiger!,' " "The White Seal," " 'Rikki-tikki-tavi,' " "Toomai of the Elephants," "The Servants of the Queen."

Just So Stories for Little Children (*JSS*). London: Macmillan and Co., 1902. "How the Whale Got His Throat," "How the Camel Got His Hump," "How the Rhinoceros Got His Skin," "How the Leopard Got His Spots," "The Elephant's Child," "The Sing-Song of Old Man Kangaroo," "The Beginning of the Armadilloes," "How the First Letter Was Written," "How the Alphabet Was Made," "The Crab that Played with the Sea," "The Cat that Walked by Himself," "The Butterfly that Stamped."

Land and Sea Tales (*L&S*). London: Macmillan and Co., Ltd., 1923. "Winning the Victoria Cross," "The Way that He Took," "An Unqualified Pilot," "His Gift," "A Flight of Fact," "Stalky," "The Burning of the Sarah Sands," "The Parable of Boy Jones," "The Bold 'Prentice," "The Son of His Father," "An English School."

Life's Handicap, Being Stories of Mine Own People (*LH*). London: Macmillan and Co., 1891. "The Incarnation of Krishna Mulvaney," "The Courting of Dinah Shadd," "On Greenhow Hill," "The Man Who Was," "The Head of the District," "Without Benefit of Clergy," "At the End of the Passage," "The Mutiny of the Mavericks," "The Mark of the Beast," "The Return of Imray," "Namgay Doola," "The Lang Men o'Larut," "Bertran and Bimi," "Reingelder and the German Flag," "The Wandering Jew," "Through the Fire," "The Finances of the Gods," "The Amir's Homily," "Jews in Shusan," "The Limitations of Pambé Serang," "Little Tobrah," "Moti-Guj—Mutineer," "Bubbling Well Road," " 'The City of Dreadful Night,' " "Georgie Porgie," "Naboth," "The Dream of Duncan Parrenness."

Limits and Renewals (*L&R*). London: Macmillan and Co., Ltd., 1932. "Dayspring Mishandled," "The Woman in His Life," "The Tie," "The Church that Was at Antioch," "Aunt Ellen," "Fairy-Kist," "A Naval Mutiny," "The Debt," "The Manner of Men," "Unprofessional," "Beauty Spots," "The Miracle of Saint Jubanus," "The Tender Achilles," "Uncovenanted Mercies."

Many Inventions (*MI*). London: Macmillan and Co., 1893. "To the True Romance," "The Disturber of Traffic," "A Conference of the Powers," "My Lord the Elephant," "One View of the Question," "The Finest Story in the World," "His Private Honour," "A Matter of Fact," "The Lost Legion," "In the Rukh," "Brugglesmith," "Love-o'-Women," "The Record of Bedalia Herodsfoot," "Judson and the Empire," "The Children of the Zodiac."

The Phantom 'Rickshaw and Other Tales (*PR*). Allahabad: A. H. Wheeler & Co., 1888. Later collected in *Wee Willie Winkie*. "The Phantom 'Rickshaw," "My Own True Ghost Story," "The Strange Ride of Morrowbie Jukes," "The Man Who Would Be King."

Plain Tales from the Hills (*PTH*). Calcutta: Thacker, Spink and Co., 1888. A few of these tales, though published in the *Civil and Military Gazette*, remained uncollected until the Outward Bound edition of *PTH* in 1897. "Lispeth," "Three and—an Extra," "Thrown Away," "Miss Youghal's *Sais*," "Bitters Neat," "'Yoked with an Unbeliever,'" "False Dawn," "The Rescue of Pluffles," "Cupid's Arrows," "The Three Musketeers," "His Chance in Life," "Watches of the Night," "The Other Man," "Haunted Subalterns," "Consequences," "The Conversion of Aurelian McGoggin," "The Taking of Lungtungpen," "A Germ-Destroyer," "Kidnapped," "The Arrest of Lieutenant Golightly," "In the House of Suddhoo," "His Wedded Wife," "The Broken-Link Handicap," "Beyond the Pale," "In Error," "A Bank Fraud," "Tods' Amendment," "The Daughter of the Regiment," "In the Pride of His Youth," "Pig," "The Rout of the White Hussars," "The Bronckhorst Divorce-Case," "Venus Annodomini," "The Bisara of Pooree," "A Friend's Friend," "The Gate of the Hundred Sorrows," "The Madness of Private Ortheris," "The

Story of Muhammad Din," "On the Strength of a Likeness," "Wressley of the Foreign Office," "By Word of Mouth," "To Be Filed for Reference."

Puck of Pook's Hill (PPH). London: Macmillan and Co., 1906. "Weland's Sword," "Young Men at the Manor," "The Knights of the Joyous Venture," "Old Men at Pevensey," "A Centurion of the Thirtieth," "On the Great Wall," "The Winged Hats," "Hal o' the Draft," " 'Dymchurch Flit,' " "The Treasure and the Law."

Rewards and Fairies (R&F). London: Macmillan and Co., Ltd., 1910. "Cold Iron," "Gloriana," "The Wrong Thing," "Marklake Witches," "The Knife and the Naked Chalk," "Brother Square-Toes," "A Priest in Spite of Himself," "The Conversion of St Wilfrid," "A Doctor of Medicine," "Simple Simon," "The Tree of Justice."

The Second Jungle Book (SJB). London: Macmillan and Co., 1895. "How Fear Came," "The Miracle of Purun Bhagat," "Letting in the Jungle," "The Undertakers," "The King's Ankus," "Quiquern," "Red Dog," "The Spring Running."

Soldiers Three (ST). Allahabad, India: The "Pioneer" Press, 1888. "God from the Machine," "Private Learoyd's Story," "The Big Drunk Draf'," "The Solid Muldoon," "With the Main Guard," "In the Matter of a Private," "Black Jack."

Stalky & Co. (S&C). London: Macmillan and Co., 1899. "In Ambush," "Slaves of the Lamp, Part 1," "An Unsavory Interlude," "The Impressionists," "The Moral Reformers," "A Little Prep," "The Flag of Their Country," "The Last Term," "Slaves of the Lamp, Part II."

The Story of the Gadsbys (SG). Allahabad, India: A. H. Wheeler & Co., 1888. Later collected in *Soldiers Three*. "Poor Dear Mamma," "The World Without," "The Tents of Kedar," "With Any Amazement," "The Garden of Eden," "Fatima," "The Valley of the Shadow," "The Swelling of the Jordan."

Traffics and Discoveries (T&D). London: Macmillan and Co., 1904. "The Captive," "The Bonds of Discipline," "A Sahibs' War," " 'Their Lawful Occasions,' " "The Comprehension of Private Copper," "Steam Tactics," " 'Wireless,' " "The Army of a Dream," " 'They,' " "Mrs Bathurst," "Below the Mill Dam."

Under the Deodars (UD). Allahabad, India: A. H. Wheeler & Co., 1888. Later collected in *Wee Willie Winkie*. "The Education of Otis Yeere," "At the Pit's Mouth," "A Wayside Comedy," "The Hill of Illusion," "A Second-Rate Woman," "Only a Subaltern."

Wee Willie Winkie and Other Child Stories (WWW). Allahabad, India: A. H. Wheeler & Co., 1888. "Wee Willie Winkie," "Baa, Baa, Black Sheep," "His Majesty the King," "The Drums of the Fore and Aft."

Secondary Works

The critical commentary available on Kipling and his works is enormous. In the following, very selective, bibliography, I have tried to suggest the variety of approaches critics have taken to Kipling as well as to list the standard and best studies.

Books and Parts of Books

Biographical

Ankers, Arthur R. *The Pater: John Lockwood Kipling, His Life and Times.* Oxford, England: Pond View, 1988.

Birkenhead, Lord. *Rudyard Kipling.* London: Weidenfeld & Nicholson, 1978.

Carrington, Charles. *Rudyard Kipling, His Life and Work.* Garden City, N.Y.: Doubleday & Company, 1955.

Gross, John, ed. *Rudyard Kipling: The Man, His Work, and His World.* London: Weidenfeld & Nicholson, 1972.

Mason, Philip. *Kipling: The Glass, the Shadow and the Fire.* New York: Harper & Row, 1975.

Wilson, Angus. *The Strange Ride of Rudyard Kipling: His Life and Works.* London: Secker & Warburg, 1977.

Critical

Bayley, John. *The Uses of Division: Unity and Disharmony in Literature.* London: Chatto and Windus, 1976.

———. *The Short Story: Henry James to Elizabeth Bowen.* New York: St. Martin's Press, 1988.

Bodelson, C. A. *Aspects of Kipling's Art.* Manchester: Manchester University Press, 1964.

Brantlinger, Patrick. *Rule of Darkness: British Literature and Imperialism, 1830–1914.* Ithaca: Cornell University Press, 1990.

Cornell, Louis. *Kipling in India.* London: Macmillan Press Ltd., 1966.

Crook, Nora. *Kipling's Myths of Love and Death.* Basingstoke: Macmillan Press Ltd., 1989.

Dobrée, Bonamy. *Rudyard Kipling: Realist and Fabulist.* London: Oxford University Press, 1967.

Eliot, T. S. "Introduction." *A Choice of Kipling's Verse.* London: Faber and Faber, Ltd., 1941.

Gilbert, B. J. Moore. *Kipling and Orientalism.* London: Croom Helm, 1986.

Gilbert, Elliot L. *The Good Kipling: Studies in the Short Story.* Oberlin: Ohio University Press, 1970.

———. *Kipling and the Critics.* New York: New York University Press, 1965.

Gish, Robert. "The Exotic Short Story: Kipling and Others." In *The English Short Story 1880–1945: A Critical History*, edited by Joseph M. Flora, 1–37. Boston: Twayne Publishers, 1985.

Green, Roger Lancelyn, ed. *Kipling: the Critical Heritage*. London: Routledge and Kegan Paul, 1971.

Greenberger, Allen J. *The British Image of India in the Literature of Imperialism 1880–1960*. London: Oxford University Press, 1969.

Hanson, Clare. *Short Stories and Short Fictions, 1880–1980*. New York: St. Martin's Press, 1985.

Harris, Wendell. *British Short Fiction in the Nineteenth Century*. Detroit: Wayne State University Press, 1979.

Haughton, Hugh. "Introduction." *Wee Willie Winkie*. London: Penguin Books, 1988.

Islam, Shamsul. *Kipling's "Law": A Study of His Philosophy of Life*. New York: St. Martin's Press, 1975.

Jarrell, Randall. *Kipling, Auden & Co.: Essays and Reviews, 1935–1964*. New York: Farrar, Strauss and Giroux, 1980.

Kamra, Sukeshi. *Kipling's Vision: A Study in His Short Stories*. New Delhi: Prestige Books, 1959.

Karlin, Daniel. "Introduction." *The Jungle Books*. London: Penguin Books, 1987.

Kemp, Sandra. *Kipling's Hidden Narratives*. Oxford: Basil Blackwell Ltd., 1988.

Lascelles, Mary. *The Story-teller Retrieves the Past: Historical Fiction and Fictitious History in the Art of Scott, Stevenson, Kipling, and Some Others*. Oxford: Clarendon Press, 1980.

McClure, John A. *Kipling and Conrad: The Colonial Fiction*. Cambridge, Mass.: Harvard University Press, 1981.

Mallett, Phillip, ed. *Kipling Considered*. Basingstoke: Macmillan Press Ltd., 1989.

Meyers, Jeffrey. *Fiction and the Colonial Experience*. Ipswich, N.H.: Boydell Press, 1973.

Orel, Harold. *A Kipling Chronology*. Boston: G. K. Hall, 1990.

———. *The Victorian Short Story: Development and Triumph of a Literary Genre*. Cambridge: Cambridge University Press, 1986.

———, ed. *Critical Essays on Rudyard Kipling*. Boston: G. K. Hall, 1989.

———, ed. *Kipling: Interviews and Recollections*. 2 vols. Totowa, N.J.: Barnes and Noble Books, 1983.

Paffard, Mark. *Kipling's Indian Fiction*. Basingstoke: Macmillan Press Ltd., 1989.

Page, Norman, ed. *A Kipling Companion*. London: Macmillan Press Ltd., 1984.

Reader's Guide to Rudyard Kipling's Works, edited by R. E. Harbord and R. L. Green. 8 vols. Canterbury: Privately printed, 1961–72.

Rutherford, Andrew, ed. *Kipling's Mind and Art*. Edinburgh and London: Oliver & Boyd, 1964.

Said, Edward W. *Orientalism*. New York: Pantheon Books, 1978.

Sandison, A. G. "Rudyard Kipling." In *British Writers*, edited by Ian Scott-Kilvert, 6:165–206. New York: Charles Scribner's Sons, 1983.

Stewart, J. I. M. *Rudyard Kipling*. New York: Dodd, Mead & Company, 1966.

Suleri, Sara. *The Rhetoric of English India*. Chicago: University of Chicago Press, 1992.

Tompkins, J. M. S. *The Art of Rudyard Kipling*. Lincoln: University of Nebraska Press, 1959.

Wilson, Edmund. "The Kipling that Nobody Read." In *The Wound and the Bow*, 105–81. New York: Oxford University Press, 1947.

Wurgraft, Lewis D. *The Imperial Imagination: Magic and Myth in Kipling's India*. Middletown, Conn.: Wesleyan University Press, 1983.

Journal Articles

Arata, Stephen D. "A Universal Foreignness: Kipling in the Fin-de-Siècle." *English Literature in Transition 1880–1920* 36 (1993): 7–38.

Bascom, Tim. "Secret Imperialism: The Reader's Response to the Narrator in 'The Man Who Would Be King.'" *English Literature in Transition 1880–1920* 31 (1988): 162–83.

Bayley, John. "The False Structure." *English Literature in Transition 1880–1920* 29 (1986): 19–27.

———. "Mrs Bathurst Again." *Essays in Criticism* 38 (1988): 233–36.

Carrington, C. E. " 'Baa, Baa, Black Sheep': Fact or Fiction." *Kipling Journal* 39 (June 1972): 7–14.

Cheff, Jim. "'With Illustrations by the Author': Some Author-Artists of the Nineteenth Century." *American Book Collector* 8 (1987): 13–19.

Coates, John. "Memories of Mansura: the 'Tints and Textures' of Kipling's Late Art in 'The Eye of Allah.' " *Modern Language Review* 85 (1990): 555–69.

———. "'Proofs of Holy Writ': Kipling's Valedictory Statement on Art." *Kipling Journal* 61 (September 1987): 12–20.

Crawford, Robert. "Rudyard Kipling in the Waste Land." *Essays in Criticism* 36 (1986): 32–46.

Gilbert, Elliot L. "Silence and Survival in Rudyard Kipling's Art and Life." *English Literature in Transition 1880–1920* 29 (1986): 115–26.

———. "What Happens in 'Mrs. Bathurst.' " *PMLA* 77 (1962): 450–58.

Lewis, L. A. F. "Some Links between the Stories in Kipling's *Debits and Credits*." *English Literature in Transition 1880–1920* 25 (1982): 74–85.

MacDonald, Robert H. "Discourse and Ideology in Kipling's 'Beyond the Pale.' " *Studies in Short Fiction* 23 (1986): 413–18.

Mason, Philip. "Two Kipling Puzzles." *Kipling Journal* 62 (September 1988): 25–34.

McBratney, John. "Imperial Subjects, Imperial Space in Kipling's *Jungle Book*." *Victorian Studies* 35 (1992): 277–93.

———. "Lovers beyond the Pale: Images of Indian Women in Kipling's Tales of Miscegenation." *Works and Days: Essays in the Socio-Historical Dimensions of Literature and the Arts* 8 (Spring 1990): 17–36.

Meyers, Jeffrey. "The Idea of Moral Authority in 'The Man Who Would Be King.'" *Studies in English Literature* 8 (1968): 711–23.

Page, Norman. "What Happens in 'Mary Postgate'?" *English Literature in Transition 1880–1920* 29 (1986): 41–37.

Parry, Ann. "Reading Formations in the Victorian Press: The Reception of Kipling 1888–1891." *Literature and History* 11 (1985): 254–63.

———. "'Take away that bauble!' Political Allegory in 'Below the Mill Dam.'" *Kipling Journal* 62 (December 1988): 10–24.

Ricketts, Harry. "'Kipling and the War: A Reading of *Debits and Credits*." *English Literature in Transition 1880–1920* 29 (1986): 29–39.

Schaub, Danielle. "Kipling's Craftsmanship in 'The Bull that Thought.'" *Studies in Short Fiction* 22 (1985): 309–16.

Scheik, William J. "Hesitation in Kipling's 'The Phantom 'Rickshaw.'" *English Literature in Transition 1880–1920* 29 (1986): 48–53.

Shippey, Thomas A. and Michael Short. "Framing and Distancing in Kipling's 'The Man Who Would Be King.'" *Journal of Narrative Technique* 2 (1972): 75–87.

Spivak, Gayatri Chakravorty. "Imperialism and Sexual Difference." *Oxford Literary Review* 8 (1986): 225–40.

Stewart, David H. "Kipling's Portraits of the Artist." *English Literature in Transition 1880–1920* 31 (1988): 265–83.

Stinton, T. C. W. "What Really Happened in 'Mrs Bathurst'?" *Essays in Criticism* 38 (1988): 55–74.

Sullivan, Zohreh T. "Kipling the Nightwalker." *Modern Fiction Studies* 30 (1984): 217–35.

Waterhouse, Ruth. "'That Blindish Look': Signification of Meaning in 'Mrs. Bathurst.'" *Studia Neophilologica* 60 (1988): 193–206.

Bibliographies

Chandler, L. H. *Summary of the Works of Rudyard Kipling.* New York: Grolier Club, 1930.

Gerber, Helmut E. and Edward Lauterbach. "Rudyard Kipling: An Annotated Bibliography of Writings about Him." *English Fiction in Transition 1880–1920* 3, nos. 3–5 (1960): 1–235.

Lauterbach, Edward. "An Annotated Bibliography of Writings about Rudyard Kipling: First Supplement." *English Literature in Transition 1880–1920* 8 (1965): 136–241.

Livingston, Flora V. *Bibliography of the Works of Rudyard Kipling.* New York: Edgar H. Wells and Company, 1927.

———. *Supplement to Bibliography of the Works of Rudyard Kipling.* New York: Burt Franklin, 1938; rpt., 1968.

Martindell, E. W. *A Bibliography of the Works of Rudyard Kipling (1881–1923).* London: John Lane, the Bodley Head Ltd., 1923.

Stewart, James McGregor. *Rudyard Kipling: A Bibliographical Catalogue*, edited by A. W. Yeats. Toronto: Dalhousie University Press, 1959.

Index

The Author

Helen Pike Bauer is associate professor of English at Iona College in New York, where she teaches courses on the English novel and the nineteenth-century novel. She has published essays on nineteenth- and twentieth-century literature, particularly on John Ruskin, Arnold Bennett, and Tillie Olsen.

The Editor

General Editor Gordon Weaver earned his B.A. in English at the University of Wisconsin-Milwaukee in 1961; his M.A. in English at the University of Illinois, where he studied as a Woodrow Wilson Fellow, in 1962; and his Ph.D. in English and creative writing at the University of Denver in 1970. He is author of several novels, including *Count a Lonely Cadence, Give Him a Stone, Circling Byzantium*, and most recently *The Eight Corners of the World* (1988). Many of his numerous short stories are collected in *The Entombed Man of Thule, Such Waltzing Was Not Easy, Getting Serious, Morality Play, A World Quite Round*, and *Men Who Would Be Good* (1991). Recognition of his fiction includes the St. Lawrence Award of Fiction (1973), two National Endowment for the Arts Fellowships (1974, 1989), and the O. Henry First Prize (1979). He edited *The American Short Story, 1945–1980: A Critical History*, and is currently editor of *Cimarron Review*. He is professor of English at Oklahoma State University. Married, and the father of three daughters, he lives in Stillwater, Oklahoma.